MEASURING PERFORMANCE

THE EARLY CHILDHOOD EDUCATOR IN PRACTICE

MEASURING PERFORMANCE
The Early Childhood Educator in Practice

FOR THOSE WHO EDUCATE AND CARE FOR YOUNG CHILDREN

Barbara Elliott, M.Ed.

DELMAR
CENGAGE Learning

Australia · Brazil · Japan · Korea · Mexico · Singapore · Spain · United Kingdom · United States

DELMAR
CENGAGE Learning

Measuring Performance: The Early Childhood Educator in Practice
Barbara Elliott

Business Unit Director:
Susan L. Simpfenderfer

Executive Editor:
Marlene McHugh Pratt

Acquisitions Editor:
Erin O Connor Traylor

Developmental Editor:
Melissa Riveglia

Editorial Assistant: **Alexis Ferraro**

Executive Production Manager:
Wendy A. Troeger

Production Editor: **Elaine Scull**

Project Editor: **Amy E. Tucker**

Technology Manager:
James Considine

Executive Marketing Manager:
Donna J. Lewis

Channel Manager:
Wendy E. Mapstone

Cover Design: **Joseph Villanova**

For product information and technology assistance, contact us at
Professional & Career Group Customer Support, 1-800-648-7450

For permission to use material from this text or product, submit all requests online at **www.cengage.com/permissions**
Further permissions questions can be emailed to
permissionrequest@cengage.com

ExamView® and ExamView Pro® are registered trademarks of FSCreations, Inc. Windows is a registered trademark of the Microsoft Corporation used herein under license. Macintosh and Power Macintosh are registered trademarks of Apple Computer, Inc. Used herein under license.

Library of Congress Control Number:

ISBN-13: 978-0-7668-4067-6

ISBN-10: 0-7668-4067-0

Delmar Cengage Learning
5 Maxwell Drive
Clifton Park, NY 12065-2919
USA

Cengage Learning products are represented in Canada by Nelson Education, Ltd.

For your lifelong learning solutions, visit **delmar.cengage.com**

Visit our corporate website at **www.cengage.com**

Notice to the Reader

Publisher does not warrant or guarantee any of the products described herein or perform any independent analysis in connection with any of the product information contained herein. Publisher does not assume, and expressly disclaims, any obligation to obtain and include information other than that provided to it by the manufacturer. The reader is expressly warned to consider and adopt all safety precautions that might be indicated by the activities described herein and to avoid all potential hazards. By following the instructions contained herein, the reader willingly assumes all risks in connection with such instructions. The publisher makes no representations or warranties of any kind, including but not limited to, the warranties of fitness for particular purpose or merchantability, nor are any such representations implied with respect to the material set forth herein, and the publisher takes no responsibility with respect to such material. The publisher shall not be liable for any special, consequential, or exemplary damages resulting, in whole or part, from the readers' use of, or reliance upon, this material.

Printed in the United States of America
5 6 7 8 9 12 11 10

Contents

Preface

EARLY CHILDHOOD EDUCATION MEANS...

Empowering children through knowledge, skills, and social values to develop capabilities of reasoning and judgment necessary to live in harmony with him/herself, the family, and the immediate and global community.

Measuring Performance can assist you, the Educator in Practice, to accomplish this goal. It recognizes the vital role of the educator supporting the learning and development of children. *Measuring Performance* is a vehicle to measure the educator's best performance critical to the optimal development of young children.

WHAT IS *MEASURING PERFORMANCE?*

Measuring Performance is an essential tool for all educators dedicated to the healthy development of young children. This book is a **self-assessment** guide for the Early Childhood Educator in Practice. It is a set of best performance standards based on knowledge, research, and experience that defines the characteristics necessary to successfully perform the expected tasks associated with the Early Childhood Education profession. These standards, compiled over time from a variety of sources, can act as a guide to self-evaluation and professional accountability.

Early Childhood professionals are looking for ways to evaluate their skills. *Measuring Performance* is an instrument to facilitate the assessment of applied theory, skills, knowledge, and abilities of those who care for and educate young children. *Measuring Performance* is a document of competencies or behaviors outlining the optimal level of practice for Early Childhood Education complete with a rating scale.

This book is intended to be used by Early Childhood Educators, demonstrating on a day-to-day basis the care and education of young children, who require a strong definition of quality in their practice. Additionally, *Measuring Performance* is extremely valuable in assessing appropriate approaches to curriculum adaptation as well as defining optimal space and materials.

As a profession establishes exemplary practice by defining a mission, vision, and code of ethics (core values), the constituents of the profession seek a way to achieve this mission, work toward the vision, and demonstrate the code of ethics. *Measuring Performance* clearly states the level of performance necessary to enhance the quality of life for young children and their families. Continuing competence can be further determined by measuring performance within the practice on an ongoing basis. It invites creative solutions, through thoughtful reflection on one's teaching practice, to recognize curriculum and environmental deficiencies.

Measuring Performance is a self-motivating plan with the goal of actualizing optimal practice in Early Childhood Education. It is an instrument to measure the skills, behaviors, and abilities of Early Childhood Educators in pursuit of excellence.

ACKNOWLEDGMENTS

I gratefully acknowledge:

- ♦ **Communities Together for Children**, Thunder Bay, Ontario, Canada, for their active involvement in editing this document. Under the able direction of Karen Fogolin, this agency made recommendations for change as well as provided the supports and resources for this to be done. A heartfelt thank you to Karen for her ongoing contribution and support.
- ♦ **The Editorial Committee**, chaired by Anita Broere. Committee members were Karen Fogolin, Gina Ruberto, Aline Black, Marnie Tarzia, and Janette Bax. They were assisted by other colleagues active in the field.
- ♦ **The Early Childhood Education Faculty and Staff of the Children and Family Centre**, Confederation College, Thunder Bay, as well as partners from the Lakehead Board of Education, Thunder Bay. Aline Black and Heather Exely contributed greatly to making this document relevant to Early Primary Teachers.

Special thanks to Valerie Rhomberg, Institute for Early Development, Mothercraft, Toronto, Canada, for her help in ensuring anti-bias sensitivity throughout the manuscript.

The author and Delmar would like to extend a special thank you to the following reviewers for their comments and recommendations:

Billie Armstrong
Greensboro College
Columbia, North Carolina

Jody Martin
Children's World Learning Centers
Golden, Colorado

Nancy Baptiste, Ed.D.
New Mexico State University
Las Cruces, New Mexico

Betty Pearsall, M.S.
Queens College
Westbury, New York

Birdena Hamilton-Armitage
Conestoga College
Kitchener, Ontario, Canada

Ann Stone
Langara College
Vancouver, British Columbia, Canada

ABOUT THE AUTHOR

Barbara Elliott, M.Ed., has worked more than three decades in the field of Early Childhood Education (E.C.E.) and has held various positions in municipal, nonprofit, and parent co-operative child care, and at a community college. Past President of the Association of Early Childhood Educators of Ontario, she was also Chair of the E.C.E. Department at Confederation College, Thunder Bay. Barbara was the recipient of the Provincial Children's Services Award for her contribution to Early Childhood Education.

Her passion has always been in developing those who work directly with young children. Using innovative approaches to the delivery of quality early childhood education, she has pressed for legislative recognition of the profession and is committed to raising community awareness of the value of early childhood education to our children and grandchildren.

Author of parent manuals, articles on multi-aged grouping, and various study guides in child development and child guidance for Confederation College Curriculum Design and Development Department, Barbara currently consults to education authorities, community agencies, and special interest groups on professional growth and development for teachers and caregivers.

Barbara and her husband have raised two children and now celebrate the lives of their grandchildren.

"It is my hope that the persons who educate and care for young children will use *Measuring Performance* to enhance their abilities and find a new vision of education and care. Supporting research shows that the quality of education and care invested in the early years can ensure that children are more socially and cognitively prepared to meet their future . . . and the main link to quality is the early childhood education, in partnerships with parents."

—Barbara Elliott

Introduction

THE COMPLEX ROLE OF THE EARLY CHILDHOOD EDUCATOR

The field of Early Childhood Education, like all other professions, distinguishes itself by requiring a specific body of knowledge necessary to fulfill the role expected by the Early Childhood professional. The complexity of the role is exacerbated by many factors.

Early Childhood Educators, in partnership with parents, have a great influence on the growth and development of young children. Research emphasizing the importance of the care and educational experiences during the child's early years commands a need for professionals capable of fulfilling a complex and multifaceted role. The importance of this role is often undervalued because child care is viewed as a charity that serves a relief function for families rather than being concerned for the developmental needs of children. The need for qualified, competent early childhood educators is critical to the future of our society.

In performing the role, the words "education" and "care" become synonymous. The functions of care and education become interchangeable. Unlike other "teaching" roles, this factor adds to the complexities of the role. Most Early Childhood Educators find themselves performing a myriad of functions in any given day when in the company of young children.

Early childhood settings include programs in a center, school, or home that serve children from birth through age 6 and their families, including children with special developmental and learning needs. Educators within these settings must play a number of different roles from decision-maker, child development expert, curriculum designer, and diagnostician to counselor, collaborator, and advisor. The theory, knowledge, and skills demonstrated by the educator provides the underpinnings required to complete the role. These diverse day-to-day requirements contribute to the intricacy of the educator's position, which must keep up with the needs of a rapidly changing society.

Child-centered curriculums now include the very young. Research focusing on infants and toddlers (for instance, research addressing the development of the brain) points to the educator acquiring specific knowledge and skills for optimal growth and care. Programs are serving families' needs for non-standard hour care. Child care has moved beyond the traditional hours to include shift work, overnight, and weekend care. The specifications required to do this job expand greatly when the attributes of working with adults are added. The implementation of family-centered services requires specific skills to work collaboratively with family members and other professionals.

The needs of diverse families are being recognized. Federal law and state/provincial initiatives have opened the doors to children with complex learning, behavioral, and developmental needs. As well, immigration has introduced a wider array of languages and cultures into child care requiring a culturally and linguistically relevant perspective. Educators are expected to capitalize on the diversity as well as the commonality that exist among all children and families. Programs are providing a wider range of services to children and families from health and nutrition to the provision of speech, physical, and occupational therapy. Thus, educators are developing cross-disciplinary approaches to the care and education of young children.

Educators of young children must develop a set of personal and professional beliefs that lead to consistency in practice. Their professional code of ethics addresses their responsibilities to children, families, colleagues, and society and must be internalized and reflected in their daily interactions with children and adults. Consistently implementing professional ethics and learning to teach is a career-long process. Establishing credentials in the field of early childhood education is just the beginning and is not enough to sustain a teacher throughout his/her career. The responsibility to grow and continually build competencies requires exemplary practices established by the profession and the commitment of educators to measure their own ability next to this set of standards. *Measuring Performance* is designed to guide the user in the pursuit of exemplary practice.

PROFESSIONAL DEVELOPMENT IN THE LIVES OF EARLY CHILDHOOD EDUCATORS

A well-known quality of an outstanding Early Childhood Educator is the effort invested in ongoing professional development. Continuing competence is clearly the single most important responsibility associated with the ongoing practice of this profession. To address this responsibility, each practitioner requires succinct feedback to his/her performance through evaluation and access to resources.

When a profession establishes exemplary practice by defining a mission, vision, and code of ethics (core values), the constituents of the profession seek a way to achieve this mission, work toward the vision, and demonstrate the code of ethics through their daily practice. Professional development is the vehicle to help this happen.

Professional development embraces self-assessment, skill renewal, and personal growth. These often neglected components combined with performance feedback provide the fertile bed for optimum ongoing competence.

The National Association for the Education of Young Children's position statement on professional development provides a comprehensive look at this issue. The following principles of professional development have been incorporated into *Measuring Performance*:

♦ Learning and growing is a lifelong process.
♦ Professional development goes beyond core knowledge to include communication, personal growth, and advocacy.
♦ Learning is most effective when it is individualized.
♦ Professionals should be involved in the planning of their professional development program.
♦ Effective professional development experiences provide opportunities for application and reflection and allow for individuals to be observed and receive feedback.

Researchers have studied the ways teachers grow from their initial exit from training to becoming mature professionals. Lillian Katz is a leading expert in this area. Her four stages of development for teachers demonstrate the increased levels of complexity.

According to Katz (1977) in **Stage 1**, teachers begin their practice with sheer **survival** in mind. The responsibility and adjustment to post-training experiences causes the teacher to look for encouragement, support, and mentoring. **Stage 2** follows with **consolidation**. Knowing that survival is possible, teachers begin to focus on specific aspects of the field. They are able to consolidate the knowledge gained from their entry to practice and move to specialized fields of study such as children with special needs. **Stage 3** brings the teacher to a need for **renewal**— looking for new approaches and becoming reacquainted with information learned but not used.

Stage 4 is **maturity**, when the teacher is ready to share his/her knowledge with others. They come to terms with their style of practice and look to the larger concept of the profession for expression and contribution.

Measuring Performance is a helpful tool for each stage of teacher development. It is a bridge to help the teacher in the **survival** stage to feel support and encouragement. It helps the teacher in **consolidation** identify the focus that suits best. This document is of great assistance to the teacher seeking **renewal of skills** as he/she completes the requirements and brings back previously learned behaviors. The **mature** teacher can use this book as a guide when interacting with a broader audience or when mentoring others.

CONTEMPORARY FINDINGS IN EARLY CHILDHOOD EDUCATION

Brain Development: Importance in the Early Years

New understanding of brain development in the early years, and its effect on subsequent learning, emotional well-being, behavior, and health of the child, has to be a high priority if we want children to reach their full potential. We now know that the development of the brain in the early years of life, particularly the first three years, sets the base for competence (what we have learned and our ability to learn) and coping skills (how we respond to challenges and handle stress) for the later stages of life.

Well-planned, age appropriate stimulation that drives and promotes the formation of connections (neurons) in the highly sensitive early years has a major effect on a child's development of cognition and behavior. Key reasoning and cognitive functions in mathematics are acquired between the ages of 4 and 7 years.

The years from conception to age 6 set a base for thinking, behavior, and health over the life cycle. The brain's great spurt draws to a close around the age of 10 years. By then, only the strongest connections of the brain will be well established. At this time, we know that the brain systems that allow us to think, feel, and act are shaped by **experience**. This means that children are deeply affected by their early experiences. Sensory stimulation (sights, sounds, touches, smells, and tastes) the brain receives during this sensitive, critical period drives the connections (neurons) changing the physical structure of the brain. An infant that senses safety and security establishes a *wiring pattern* in the brain that can reduce anxiety and allow the brain to better absorb and incorporate new sensory stimulation.

This powerful research on the development of the human brain compels top-level decision-makers to take action. The development of the whole child that will lead to scholastic, career, and social success is so important that educators, health care professionals, social service leaders, and politicians are beginning to establish policy that will improve the current status of young children and their families.

The synthesis of neuroscience, developmental psychology, sociology, and the determinants of health, learning, and economic growth is coming together to establish a framework of understanding. These insights will help us know how the early years of child development affect our learning behavior and health throughout the life cycle. This knowledge emphasizes the need for a continuing focus on the parent and child for optimum brain development in the early years.

Information to assist the Early Childhood Educator has been integrated into *Measuring Performance* as they perform their daily practice. A young child's relationship with parents, early childhood educators, and other significant caregivers affects the way a child's brain develops. It is, therefore, of extreme importance that we incorporate this knowledge into practice.

SELF-ASSESSMENT/REFLECTION AND ACTION PLANNING AS IMPORTANT ASPECTS OF PROFESSIONAL DEVELOPMENT

Educators of young children find themselves busy with lists, plans, and responsibilities that are inherent with the role. Reflecting and assessing skills are often at the bottom of the list. Self-assessment is a vital link to our personal and professional development. Yet, it is a neglected and difficult task to complete without a measurement tool or set of standards to guide us. The challenges of self-evaluation are many. It is, however, seen to be an important precursor to professionalism.

Early Childhood Educators are looking for ways to evaluate or assess their own skills. This is difficult without a measuring guide. A **standard of practice** for their performance is necessary to perform the task. *Measuring Performance* provides an extensive set of standards to assist in successful **self-assessment**.

HOW TO USE *MEASURING PERFORMANCE*

Measuring Performance is divided into three sections:

    Section I: Knowledge, Interaction, Communication
    Section II: Curriculum: Review, Development, Implementation
    Section III: Preparing the Physical Environment

The person electing to use this book (Candidate) selects a Learning Partner when possible. Although it isn't essential to use a Learning Partner, this is an integral part of this evaluation procedure as it introduces peer review. Please see "What is a Learning Partner?" (page xvi) for more information.

Each section consists of an **ANCHOR STATEMENT**, or grounding statement, followed by a comprehensive list of **DEMONSTRATED BEHAVIORS** that state a measure of quality education and care for young children.

The listed **BEHAVIORS** are supported by **TASKS**. These tasks explain *how* the educator will *demonstrate* the determined behaviors.

Many of the tasks are explained by **EXAMPLES**. These examples serve to clarify the intention of the task necessary to achieve the desired behavior.

Each task is assigned a **CHECKLIST**. The checklist offers an efficient mechanism to measure the individual's response to each task. The response is categorized using terms such as **frequently, occasionally, seldom,**[1] or **yes, no, not applicable.** Comments in the column entitled **ACTION** are encouraged.

To realize the full benefit of this self-assessment guide, it is strongly recommended that each page in Section I, Section II, and Section III be read starting with the **ANCHOR STATEMENT** and **DEMONSTRATED BEHAVIORS**. This will serve as a constant reminder that the **Anchor Statement** is the base of the endeavor; the **Demonstrated Behavior** is the action expected to

---

[1] **Frequently:** Behaviors you perform automatically. Part of your usual practice of skills. You perform the behavior almost without thinking.

Occasionally: Behaviors that are part of your practice but that you sometimes don't perform. You know you do them, but sometimes you don't.

Seldom: Behaviors you usually don't perform whether you **know** you should or not.

commit to the **Anchor Statement**, and the **Tasks** are the methods that can be used to reach the desired behavior.

Candidates **review or assess** their professional and personal skills using the **DEMONSTATED BEHAVIORS** or goals outlined in this book. Each goal is considered in response to the needs of the individual. An *action plan* is created to identify each goal and the steps necessary to meet the goal. Hence the action plan is a working document to assist the candidate in continuing their professional development. **Implementing** the **Action Plan** brings further opportunity to review, reflect, and assess behaviors.

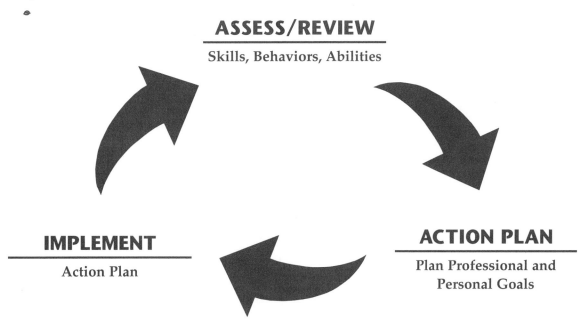

ASSESS/REVIEW

Skills, Behaviors, Abilities

ACTION PLAN

Plan Professional and Personal Goals

IMPLEMENT

Action Plan

There are three stages to using *Measuring Performance*. The stages are cyclical.

Stage I: Assessment/Review
Stage II: Action Plan (see Appendix I)
Stage III: Implementation

Following the **Implementation** stage, the user returns to the **Review** stage to determine growth and success.

STAGE I: Assessment/Review

1. The Candidate, after becoming familiar with the contents of *Measuring Performance*, will complete the checklist assigned to each of the tasks using the recommended rating system.

2. The same checklist should be completed by one or two other persons (Learning Partners) who are familiar with the recommended behaviors and the performance of the candidate.

STAGE II: Action Plan

1. The Candidate then compares the results of the exercise with the Learning Partner(s) and determines differences and commonalities.

2. This forms the basis of an **action plan**, working toward optimal performance.

3. The action plan will address the goals necessary to promote the candidate's pursuit of excellence. The goals will include necessary supports and time lines.

STAGE III: Implementation

1. The Implementation stage puts the performance plan into action. The Candidate, with the necessary support, will use the list of goals and select professional development that will successfully meet those goals.

2. At a predetermined time interval, the Candidate and the Learning Partners will review the goals and assess professional and personal success. This review will require a second completion of the checklist (using the same form with an alternate color of ink). Changes will be noted.

This procedure ensures continuing competence as the educator develops new strengths and skills in the pursuit of high-quality education and care for young children.

WHAT IS A LEARNING PARTNER?

A **Learning Partner** is chosen by the Candidate. The process of using a Learning Partner activates the peer review component of self-evaluation.

This partner(s) should be a person who is well acquainted with the work (a colleague is a recommended choice) of the candidate, a person whose observations and opinions are respected by the Candidate.

There are three ways to choose a Learning Partner:

1. Choose **two** persons, both of whom will give their honest, unbiased view of the professional performance of the Candidate. Their assessment would then be reviewed as a team with an action plan written as a result of the findings. This would include the self-evaluation completed by the Candidate.

2. Choose **one** person who would follow the procedure outlined in #1.

3. Choose multiple Learning Partners who separately know a portion of the work of the Candidate. This group would collectively provide the feedback necessary to facilitate the goals chosen by the Candidate for his/her action plan.

The need for honest, constructive opinions based on trust and mutual respect symbolizes the success of this relationship. Because the Candidate is requesting the assistance of the Learning Partner, this should presuppose the nature of this partnership.

The Learning Partner, working with his/her own copy of the checklists from the book, would make notes in the column entitled **ACTION**.

 The accompanying CD-ROM includes all the appendices. You can easily download and/or print the Appendix Checklists to use in your day-to-day practice.

DEMONSTRATED BEHAVIORS

WHAT ARE DEMONSTRATED BEHAVIORS?

Demonstrated Behaviors are a comprehensive list of behaviors, gathered from many years of empirical study, that demonstrate a measure of quality education and care for young children. This list encapsulates optimal professional and personal goals envisioned (identified) when performing the role of an Early Childhood Educator.

WHAT IS THE VALUE OF DEMONSTRATED BEHAVIORS?

The reader is able to review this list at the beginning of the assessment process, thereby knowing the scope and direction the review will take.

These **Demonstrated Behaviors** are supported by tasks deemed necessary to perform the behaviors and reach the suggested goal of optimal performance.

DEMONSTRATED BEHAVIORS

SECTION I:
Knowledge (K), Interaction (I), Communication (C)

> ✳ **The Early Childhood Educator will demonstrate a commitment to the education and care of young children through Knowledge, Interaction, and Communication in partnership with the family.**

I Will:

1. Demonstrate a current background knowledge of child development and the education of young children. K

2. Apply in practice an understanding of the characteristics of children at different levels of development. K

3. Utilize knowledge of children within a group setting to employ optimal group experiences (i.e., Homogeneous or Heterogeneous grouping). K, I

4. Employ observation as a tool for documenting children's interest and developmental levels maximizing experiences that invite participation and encourage growth. K

5. Demonstrate respect for the diversity of individuals. I

6. Build relationships with children and guide behavior toward the goal of self-discipline within a social context. I

7. Maintain a professional image. C

8. Recognize the recommended optimal teacher/child ratios and group sizes. I

9. Demonstrate knowledge of health and safety. K

10. Establish positive relationships, focusing on a comprehensive system of communication with **Families**.

    10.1 Maintain regular communications, written and oral, with families. C

    10.2 Develop useful learning experiences for families. K

    10.3 Create opportunities for relevant activities. I

    10.4 Support and encourage parents in their role. I

    10.5 Provide parents opportunities for ongoing formal/informal evaluation of their child's care and education. C

    10.6 Be aware of the responsibilities and mandates of the Board of Directors/School Advisory Committees, Child Care Owners. C

11. Establish positive relationships, focusing on a comprehensive system of communication with **Colleagues**.

11.1	Seek understanding of self to better understand the needs of others.	I
11.2	Take opportunity for effective professional development.	K
11.3	Support and encourage one another in the role.	I
11.4	Schedule meetings with colleagues regularly or as needed.	C
11.5	Schedule opportunities to discuss current and established Early Childhood Education practices.	K
11.6	Demonstrate awareness of all operating policies.	K
11.7	Demonstrate involvement in community/provincial/state Early Childhood Education-related professional associations.	K

12. Establish positive relationships, focusing on a comprehensive system of communication with the **Community**.

12.1	Network with other child-related agencies as required.	C
12.2	Participate in relevant projects or committees in the Community.	C
12.3	Promote quality child care within the Community.	C

SECTION II:
Curriculum: Review, Development, Implementation

 The Early Childhood Educator will demonstrate a commitment to the Review, Development, and Implementation of curriculum with a focus on play and experiential learning.

I Will:

1. Facilitate effective planning reflecting the observed developmental needs of all children.

2. Facilitate the emergence of skills and knowledge in each of the following domains:

2.1 COGNITIVE DOMAIN:

2.1.1 Promote spontaneity, curiosity, and discovery learning, indoors and outdoors.

2.1.2 Plan experiences to encourage the child to initiate self-directed learning experiences.

2.1.3 Provide a range of opportunities for children to explore and demonstrate critical thinking and reasoning skills.

2.1.4 Provide a range of opportunities for children to explore construction and manipulation of the environment through appropriate play experiences.

2.1.5 Promote an understanding of early mathematics.

2.1.6 Promote an understanding of early science concepts.

2.1.7 Promote an understanding of technological pursuits as they apply to the child's world.

2.2 AESTHETIC/CREATIVE DOMAIN:

2.2.1 Establish a climate for the child to explore, enjoy, and develop competence in the arts using a range of materials (see Section III).

2.2.2 Promote the use of equipment in a variety of ways.

2.2.3 Promote dramatic play to encourage fantasy, imitation, role playing, and dramatizing.

2.2.4 Promote an appreciation of beauty in nature and the arts.

2.3 AFFECTIVE DOMAIN:

2.3.1 Promote feelings of confidence and self-worth.

2.4 LANGUAGE/LITERACY DOMAIN:

2.4.1 Sustain and extend a positive attitude toward the development and use of language, both receptive and expressive, as a vehicle for learning.

2.4.2 Provide an opportunity for the development of early writing skills.

2.4.3 Provide an opportunity for children to develop early reading skills.

2.4.4 Provide appropriate language models and verbal interactions.

2.5 SOCIAL DOMAIN:

2.5.1 Establish a climate in which children can learn aspects of social skills development and experience healthy social interactions.

2.5.2 Promote a socially competent pro-social environment reflecting respect, kindness, and compassion for others.

2.6 PHYSICAL DOMAIN:

2.6.1 Promote health and safety requirements.

2.6.2 Promote appropriate nutrition requirements.

2.6.3 Promote fine and gross motor skills both indoors and outdoors.

3. Review child's progress in relation to the developmental continuum and individual goals.

3.1 Evaluate program activities weekly/monthly.

3.2 Use observation to review the emphasis in curriculum areas as well as goals for the individual child.

SECTION III:
Preparing the Physical Environment for Learning

 The Early Childhood Educator will demonstrate a commitment to Preparing the Environment for Learning.

I Will:

1. Organize the physical setting to maximize the achievements of educational/developmental goals and needs of children.

2. Equip the space to provide diverse materials necessary for holistic learning to occur in all domains.

    2.1 Cognitive Domain

    2.2 Aesthetic/Creative Domain

    2.3 Affective Domain

    2.4 Language/Literacy Domain

    2.5 Social Domain

    2.6 Physical Domain

3. Maintain physical space to ensure children's growth and encourage respect for property.

4. Establish a Community focus that encourages inclusivity and partnerships.

SECTION I:

Knowledge, Interaction, Communication

DEMONSTRATED BEHAVIORS

 The Early Childhood Educator will demonstrate a commitment to the education and care of young children through Knowledge, Interaction, and Communication in partnership with the family.

I Will:

1. Demonstrate a current background knowledge of child development and the education of young children. — K

2. Apply in practice an understanding of the characteristics of children at different levels of development. — K

3. Utilize knowledge of children within a group setting to employ optimal group experiences (i.e., Homogeneous or Heterogeneous grouping). — K, I

4. Employ observation as a tool for documenting children's interest and developmental levels maximizing experiences that invite participation and encourage growth. — K

5. Demonstrate respect for the diversity of individuals. — I

6. Build relationships with children and guide behavior toward the goal of self-discipline within a social context. — I

7. Maintain a professional image. — C

8. Recognize the recommended optimal teacher/child ratios and group sizes. — I

9. Demonstrate knowledge of health and safety. — K

10. Establish positive relationships, focusing on a comprehensive system of communication with **Families**.

   10.1 Maintain regular communications, written and oral, with families. — C

   10.2 Develop useful learning experiences for families. — K

   10.3 Create opportunities for relevant activities. — I

   10.4 Support and encourage parents in their role. — I

   10.5 Provide parents opportunities for ongoing formal/informal evaluation of their child's care and education. — C

   10.6 Be aware of responsibilities and mandates of the Board of Directors/ School Advisory Committees, Child Care Owners. — C

11. Establish positive relationships, focusing on a comprehensive system of communication with **Colleagues**.

   11.1 Seek understanding of self to better understand the needs of others. — I

11.2   Take opportunity for effective professional development.   K

11.3   Support and encourage one another in the role.   I

11.4   Schedule meetings with colleagues regularly or as needed.   C

11.5   Schedule opportunities to discuss current and established
           Early Childhood Education practices.   K

11.6   Demonstrate awareness of all operating policies.   K

11.7   Demonstrate involvement in community/provincial/state
           Early Childhood Education-related professional associations.   K

12.   Establish positive relationships, focusing on a comprehensive system of
          communication with the **Community**.

12.1   Network with other child-related agencies as required.   C

12.2   Participate in relevant projects or committees in the Community.   C

12.3   Promote quality child care within the Community.   C

CHECKLIST

> **The Early Childhood Educator will demonstrate a commitment to the education and care of young children through Knowledge, Interaction, and Communication in partnership with the family.**

I Will:

1. **Demonstrate a current background knowledge of child development and the education of young children.**

TASKS	Y	N	N/A	ACTION
1.1 Thoroughly review the principles and theories of child development annually.				
1.2 Attend Early Childhood Education-related learning experiences annually.				

2. **Apply in practice an understanding of the characteristics of children at different levels of development.**

TASKS	Y	N	N/A	ACTION
2.1 Review annually the foundation principles of Early Childhood Education. (APPENDIX A)				
2.2 Using observation and accumulated knowledge, complete a developmental checklist for individual children in assigned groups within four months of program entry. (APPENDIX B)				
2.3 Complete a profile[1] of each child including additional information.				

(continued)

---

[1] *Profile: a brief overview of child's development including:*
a) Summary of Checklist (point 2.2)
b) Observations
c) Cultural Differences
d) Other Involvement
e) General Information

Y = Yes   N = No   N/A = Not Applicable

The Early Childhood Educator will demonstrate a commitment to the education and care of young children through Knowledge, Interaction, and Communication in partnership with the family.

I Will:

2.   **Apply in practice an understanding of the characteristics of children at different levels of**

TASKS	Y	N	N/A	ACTION
2.4 Capitalize on child's natural tendency to explore and be curious by using these times to facilitate discovery learning. *Ex: The child discovers a spider. The teacher follows the child's lead and encourages the child to explore and ask questions.*				
	F	**O**	**S**	
2.5 Be flexible and intuitive to the interests and needs of individual children. *Ex. Child wants to talk about personal interests during group time. The teacher balances this child's attention interests with the goals of the whole group.*				
2.6 Engage in child's lead during conversations and activities. *Ex. A group of children playing in the sandbox with trucks decide to make a farm. The teacher assists them by providing materials to expand their learning.*				
2.7 Recognize and respond to the wide range of differences in the language development in children, for instance: 1) Sentence length 2) Use of words—e.g., tense 3) Clarity 4) Social language—e.g., please, thank you. 5) E.S.L. (English as a Second Language)				
2.8 Understand the importance of the child's separation from family and respond appropriately. *Ex. Ritual or special attention when child says goodbye to parent.*				

Y = Yes   N = No   N/A = Not Applicable   F = Frequently   O = Occasionally   S = Seldom

The Early Childhood Educator will demonstrate a commitment to the education and care of young children through Knowledge, Interaction, and Communication in partnership with the family.

I Will:

3. Utilize knowledge of children within a group setting to employ optimal group experiences (i.e., Homogeneous or Heterogeneous grouping).

TASKS	Y	N	N/A	ACTION
3.1 Facilitate multiaged/multiability group experiences (heterogeneous) to promote the interactive opportunities for social development.				
3.2 Facilitate same age groups (homogeneous) to expand learning experiences. *Ex. Cognitive learning.*				
3.3 Facilitate experiences that recognize the diverse needs of all children.				
3.4 Facilitate experiences that include the children's cultural differences.				

4. Employ observation as a tool for documenting children's interest and developmental levels maximizing experiences that invite participation and encourage growth.

TASKS	F	O	S	ACTION
4.1 Extend invitation to families and/or caregivers to observe with the educator.				
4.2 Observe and record children's interests: a) on an ongoing basis to determine emphasis in curriculum areas and goals for individual children. b) at the beginning of the year to ensure for appropriate planning for the children. c) prior to parent/teacher meetings.				
4.3 Use a curriculum planning model that includes regular observation as a method of determining developmental levels and unique interests of the children.				

Y = Yes   N = No   N/A = Not Applicable   F = Frequently   O = Occasionally   S = Seldom

The Early Childhood Educator will demonstrate a commitment to the education and care of young children through Knowledge, Interaction, and Communication in partnership with the family.

I Will:

5. Demonstrate respect for the diversity of individuals.

TASKS	F	O	S	ACTION
5.1 Become familiar with the *known* cultural experiences of each child through an initial visit and dialogue with child's family.				
5.2 Use physical body language that is welcoming and encourages interaction. *Ex. John came into the room and he wanted to tell me about his birthday party. I bent down to his eye level and said, "I'd love to hear about your party, John."*				
5.3 Offer encouragement for individual endeavors. *Ex. "You zipped your zipper up by yourself; you must feel proud of yourself."*				
5.4 Express appreciation for a child's creative endeavors by recognizing his/her efforts, e.g., block structure, artwork, necklace.				
5.5 Actively participate with the children at a developmentally appropriate level. *Ex. Assist children in becoming part of a group. I could see that Maria was wanting to get involved in the dramatic play (bus ride), so I said, "Maria, let's go over and ask if we can go for a bus ride."*				
5.6 Actively respond to child's ideas. *Ex. Ari builds a tent with blankets. The teacher asks if he would like some materials, thereby inviting expansion of this play to a camp site.*				
5.7 Encourage participation from the children. *Ex. The teacher was reading a book to the children. Tom and Susan came out of the locker room and the teacher said, "We are reading a book about trucks and cars. Would you like to join us?"*				

(continued)

F = Frequently   O = Occasionally   S = Seldom

✳ **The Early Childhood Educator will demonstrate a commitment to the education and care of young children through Knowledge, Interaction, and Communication in partnership with the family.**

5. **Demonstrate respect for the diversity of individuals.** *(continued)*

TASKS	F	O	S	ACTION
5.8 Give physical attention responsive to child's needs. *Ex. Andrew was feeling lonely when his mother left. I put my arm around him and invited him to help me set out the paint jars.*				
5.9 Encourage conversation by using open-ended questions and encouraging self-expression. *Ex. "Jose, I wonder why your block tower is tipping over?"*				
5.10 Use voice to convey expression, interest, concern, and enthusiasm. *Ex. The teacher bends down to the child's level and shows concern as the child tells him/her about his/her problem.*				
5.11 Acknowledge, respect, and respond to the child's right to have thoughts and emotions, helping the child express difficult feelings. *Ex. A child is upset when his/her Dad left. The teacher responds with a hug, "You look sad. You miss your Dad."*				
5.12 Encourage self-help skills. *Ex. Ben calls out, "I can't do this dumb zipper." The teacher said, "Sometimes these zippers can be tricky. I'll start it for you and you can do the rest."*				
5.13 Share the child's daily experiences and positive qualities with the family. *Ex. Andres really spent a long time at the water table. He took turns playing with the water wheel with Ming Lee.*				
5.14 Recognize and provide for private play when needed.				
5.15 Share ideas and feelings with children in a positive manner. *Ex. "I will be glad when the rain stops so we can go outdoors."*				

F = Frequently   O = Occasionally   S = Seldom

The Early Childhood Educator will demonstrate a commitment to the education and care of young children through Knowledge, Interaction, and Communication in partnership with the family.

I Will:

6. Build relationships with children and guide behavior toward the goal of self-discipline within a social context.

	TASKS	F	O	S	ACTION
6.1	Give children meaningful choices to encourage a sense of independence. *Ex. The teacher asked Lee, "Do you want to paint or play in the play house?"*				
6.2	Give children opportunities to self-plan and reflect, with support from the teacher. *Ex. Teacher: "You think about the places you would like to play today and we will make a plan together."*				
6.3	Use positively stated, clear directions. *Ex. When a child began throwing sand, the teacher said, "Please keep the sand in the sandbox."*				
6.4	Maintain basic limits (child not allowed to harm himself, others, animals, or property). *Ex. Dhawa pushed Jean Paul off his chair as he was going to sit down for a snack. The teacher restated the limit by saying, "Dhawa, you cannot push Jean Paul. You can tell him that you were going to sit there."*				
6.5	Develop an understanding of limits by asking children to talk about what and why these limits are important. *Ex. "What does it feel like when you are hurt?"*				

(continued)

F = Frequently   O = Occasionally   S = Seldom

The Early Childhood Educator will demonstrate a commitment to the education and care of young children through Knowledge, Interaction, and Communication in partnership with the family.

6. **Build relationships with children and guide behavior toward the goal of self-discipline within a social context.** *(continued)*

	TASKS	F	O	S	ACTION
6.6	Let children know in advance when transitions are to occur. *Ex. "Soon it will be tidy-up time," said the teacher.*				
6.7	Use effective encouragement to reinforce pro-social behavior and reciprocity. *Ex. Fernando fell and started to cry. Sophia ran to get a tissue. The teacher said, "That was very kind of you to help Fernando."*				
6.8	Assist children to understand the logical consequences of behavior and provide positive follow-up to actions. *Ex. Sam threw the paint across the table. The teacher said, "Sam, this paint needs to be cleaned up; you can get the cloth."*				
6.9	Ensure that the child experiences natural consequences to augment the opportunity for positive choices. *Ex. The teacher said, "You can put your mittens on when your hands feel cold."*				
6.10	Step in before play deteriorates and redirect the children to appropriate outlets. *Ex. Taylor and Doug pretended that they were Superman and started running around the room. The teacher said, "Come over to the rebounder and see if Superman can jump off it."*				

(continued)

F = Frequently   O = Occasionally   S = Seldom

The Early Childhood Educator will demonstrate a commitment to the education and care of young children through Knowledge, Interaction, and Communication in partnership with the family.

I Will:

6. **Build relationships with children and guide behavior toward the goal of self-discipline within a social context.** *(continued)*

	TASKS	F	O	S	ACTION
6.11	Explain realistic expectations. Follow through with those for a group or individual. *Ex. The teacher showed Jonathon the lockers and explained to him that this was where he could hang up his jacket.*				
6.12	Respond to facial and body language. *Ex. "I see you're really excited about the bubbles."*				
6.13	Assist children to utilize problem-solving skills. *Ex. Rodrigo appeared frustrated as he was unable to stack the blocks on top of each other to build a tall tower. The teacher walked over and said, "I wonder why your tower is tipping?" The teacher then asked Rodrigo if he would like some help in how to place the blocks.*				
6.14	Show respect for child's effort. *Ex. "You have worked very hard at that puzzle."*				
6.15	Use active listening to respond to children's needs. *Ex. "You sound very angry with Joel."*				
6.16	Facilitate smooth transitions between routines and throughout the day. *Ex. "Everyone who is wearing red can go to lunch time now."*				

(continued)

F = Frequently   O = Occasionally   S = Seldom

The Early Childhood Educator will demonstrate a commitment to the education and care of young children through Knowledge, Interaction, and Communication in partnership with the family.

6. **Build relationships with children and guide behavior toward the goal of self discipline within a social context.** *(continued)*

TASKS	F	O	S	ACTION
6.17 Allow child to self-adjust their behavior. *Ex. Tony has just grabbed Alan's truck. Alan takes the truck back saying "I'm still playing with it." The teacher observes this without intervening.*				
6.18 Respond immediately to child about behavior when necessary. *Ex. "Tony, if you want the truck, tell Alan to let you know when he is finished."*				
6.19 Use constructive positive language when responding to children's behavior. *Ex. "Can you think of another way to ask Jack to play with you?"*				
6.20 Follow through on stated consequences immediately. *Ex. "When you throw the sand, that shows me you are all finished. You can come with me and decide what you would like to do."*				
6.21 Implement limits and consequences consistently and with sensitivity. *Ex. "Fatima told you she didn't want you to paint on her picture. Think about what you would like to do while you are waiting to paint."*				
6.22 Support child's self assertion. *Ex. Jennifer says "I don't want to play that game." Teacher responds, "What would you rather do?"*				
6.23 Refer to Guidance Checklist. (APPENDIX C)				

F = Frequently   O = Occasionally   S = Seldom

The Early Childhood Educator will demonstrate a commitment to the education and care of young children through Knowledge, Interaction, and Communication in partnership with the family.

I Will:

7.   **Maintain a professional image.**

TASKS		Y	N	N/A	ACTION
7.1	Follow established dress code.				
7.2	Act as a language model by: ♦ using correct grammar ♦ avoiding slang terms—e.g., "you guys"				
7.3	Observe effective time management.				
7.4	Respect confidences in accordance with established policy.				
7.5	Maintain personal, physical, and emotional well-being to display energy and enthusiasm.				
7.6	Model appropriate self-control.				
7.7	Model an acceptable standard of writing. *Ex. Grammar, spelling, and format.*				
7.8	Use effective language to demonstrate fluency. *Ex. Concise, factual, comprehensive, and objective language.*				
7.9	Observe professional boundaries when communicating to children (e.g., referring to yourself as "I" rather than your name).				

Y = Yes   N = No   N/A = Not Applicable

The Early Childhood Educator will demonstrate a commitment to the education and care of young children through Knowledge, Interaction, and Communication in partnership with the family.

I Will:

8.   Recognize the recommended optimal teacher/child ratios and group sizes.

Recommendations[1] for Teacher-Child Ratios Within Different Group Sizes						
Group Size[2]	1 to 18 Months	18 to 36 Months	3 Years	4 to 5 Years	5 to 6 Years	6 to 9 Years
6	1:3[3]					
8						
10						
12		1:6				
14						
16			1:8			
18						1:18
20				1:10		
22						
25					2:25	2:25

[1] *Alter with the needs of children.*
[2] *In mixed-age groupings, the teacher-child ratio and group size should be based on the age of the majority of children in the group. However, if there are infants, ratios and group sizes for infants should be maintained at all times.*
[3] *The ratios assume that the teachers are full-time in the program. If they have other duties such as administration or parent interviewing, an additional teacher should be present to maintain the ratios.*

Source: Bredecamp, Sue, & Copple, Carol (Eds.). (1997). *Developmentally appropriate practice in early childhood programs* (page 80). Washington, DC: National Association for the Education of Young Children.

9.   **Demonstrate knowledge of health and safety.**

	TASKS	Y	N	N/A	ACTION
9.1	Maintain a valid First Aid qualification.				
9.2	Demonstrate awareness of sanitary practices. **Ex.** *Hand washing.*				
9.3	Demonstrate awareness of recognized Safety Standards. **Ex.** *crib standards.*				
9.4	Demonstrate awareness of fire evacuation procedure.				
9.5	Maintain infant/child C.P.R.				

Y = Yes   N = No   N/A = Not Applicable

The Early Childhood Educator will demonstrate a commitment to the education and care of young children through Knowledge, Interaction, and Communication in partnership with the family.

I Will:

10. **Establish positive relationships, focusing on a comprehensive system of communication with Families.**

   10.1   **Maintain regular communications, written and oral, with families.**

TASKS	Y	N	N/A	ACTION
10.1.1 Distribute a monthly newsletter to each family in the program.				
10.1.2 Inform families of relevant information regarding their child. *Ex. Accident or illness.*				
10.1.3 Document information regarding child's activities for daily living using infant/toddler report forms. (APPENDIX D)				
10.1.4 Share the completed profile (Section I, 2.3) and Checklist (Section I, 2.2) with the families.				
10.1.5 Through the newsletter, parents will be provided with a written follow-up regarding staff professional development.				
10.1.6 Inform families when absent for Professional Development. Provide the name of the replacement teacher and a brief introductory biographical sentence. Replacement teacher will introduce self to parents.				
10.1.7 Inform families of volunteers/ students taking part in the program.				
10.1.8 Demonstrate sensitivity to differing family dynamics and cultural diversity.				
10.1.9 Report and initial any extraordinary incidents in the log book.[1]				

[1] *Log Book: A daily reporting system to identify any extraordinary occurrences observed by the staff regarding children, parents, or physical space.*

Y = Yes   N = No   N/A = Not Applicable

(continued)

> **The Early Childhood Educator will demonstrate a commitment to the education and care of young children through Knowledge, Interaction, and Communication in partnership with the family.**

10.	Establish positive relationships, focusing on a comprehensive system of communication with Families.

10.1   Maintain regular communications, written and oral, with families. *(continued)*

	TASKS	Y	N	N/A	ACTION
10.1.10	Share positive attributes with parents about their child's day during daily interactions.				
10.1.11	Discuss changes in child's behavior with parents. This discussion will outline only what has been observed without judgments attached. This conversation will be documented by staff. *Ex. Teacher to parent, "We are noticing a change in Amy's behavior here at the Center."*				
10.1.12	Plan parent-teacher interviews (two times annually).				
10.1.13	Demonstrate spontaneous parent-teacher talks.				
10.1.14	Contribute to monthly newsletters for parents.				
10.1.15	Make a minimum of one initial home visit for every child (annually), being respectful of families' wishes.				
10.1.16	Demonstrate positive communication styles conducive to building trusting relations. *Ex. Active listening "I" messages; positive problem-solving skills.*				

(continued)

Y = Yes   N = No   N/A = Not Applicable

The Early Childhood Educator will demonstrate a commitment to the education and care of young children through Knowledge, Interaction, and Communication in partnership with the family.

I Will:

10.	Establish positive relationships, focusing on a comprehensive system of communication with Families.

10.1 Maintain regular communications, written and oral, with families. *(continued)*

	TASKS	Y	N	N/A	ACTION
10.1.17	Maintain and communicate policies that: a) reflect child-centered philosophy and are stated in understandable, practical terms. Policies will be clear, consistent, and respectful. *Ex. "A completed medical form and an updated inoculation is required prior to your child's entry."* b) will be distributed to each family upon admission. Updates will accompany policies as necessary.				
10.1.18	Provide alternate forms of communication to families who speak a language other than English or communicate in other than usual written forms (e.g., Braille).				

10.2 Develop useful learning experiences for families.

	TASKS	Y	N	N/A	ACTION
10.2.1	Plan a registration event for new families annually. Philosophy and policies will be clearly outlined.				
10.2.2	Participate in an Open House annually.				
10.2.3	Plan Parent evenings to address areas of interest/concern regarding family-related issues. Three evenings per year.				
10.2.4	Inform families about the availability of the resource and support systems including workshops, print resources, toy library. Post relevant information in regular newsletter.				

Y = Yes   N = No   N/A = Not Applicable

(continued)

❋ **The Early Childhood Educator will demonstrate a commitment to the education and care of young children through Knowledge, Interaction, and Communication in partnership with the family.**

10.	Establish positive relationships, focusing on a comprehensive system of communication with Families.

10.2 Develop useful learning experiences for families. *(continued)*

	TASKS	Y	N	N/A	ACTION
10.2.5	Provide families with relevant resources/information. Bulletin boards with information will be changed monthly (e.g., health related, guidance, resources video).				

10.3 Create opportunities for relevant activities.

	TASKS	Y	N	N/A	ACTION
10.3.1	Plan events for small groups of families together with teacher/educators. *Ex. Prepared or pot luck dinners. (Special holidays)*				
10.3.2	Plan special events to include all families and educators/teachers. *Ex. Seasonal carnivals.*				

10.4 Support and encourage parents in their role.

	TASKS	Y	N	N/A	ACTION
10.4.1	Provide opportunity for families to attend formal or informal support groups.				
10.4.2	Provide daily supportive interactions at beginning and/or end of day.				
10.4.3	Demonstrate an understanding of the societal trends/changes that impact the family. *Ex.* ◆ *A reflection on some of the pressures of family life.* ◆ *Flexibility in program outlines to appreciate the needs of the family.*				

Y = Yes   N = No   N/A = Not Applicable

The Early Childhood Educator will demonstrate a commitment to the education and care of young children through Knowledge, Interaction, and Communication in partnership with the family.

I Will:

10.	Establish positive relationships, focusing on a comprehensive system of communication with Families.

10.5 Provide parents opportunities for ongoing formal/informal evaluation of their child's care and education.

TASKS		Y	N	N/A	ACTION
10.5.1	Provide evaluation form for written comments.				
10.5.2	Invite families together with staff to observe the program.				

10.6 Be aware of the responsibilities and mandates of the Board of Directors/School Advisory Committees, Child Care Owners.

TASKS		Y	N	N/A	ACTION
10.6.1	Provide information to families regarding program-related boards and committees emphasizing the value of parent involvement.				
10.6.2	Access minutes of Advisory Committee and/or Board of Directors/School Council.				
10.6.3	Facilitate a process to enable parents to be aware of Board/Committee activity— e.g., access to minutes to meetings.				

11. Establish positive relationships, focusing on a comprehensive system of communication with Colleagues.

11.1 Seek understanding of self to better understand the needs of others.

TASKS		Y	N	N/A	ACTION
11.1.1	Request a performance appraisal completed by supervisor/principal (annually).				
11.1.2	Complete a self-appraisal to: a) identify personal qualities that underlie successful				

Y = Yes   N = No   N/A = Not Applicable

(continued)

> ✳ **The Early Childhood Educator will demonstrate a commitment to the education and care of young children through Knowledge, Interaction, and Communication in partnership with the family.**

11.	Establish positive relationships, focusing on a comprehensive system of communication with Colleagues.

11.1 Seek understanding of self to better understand the needs of others. *(continued)*

	TASKS	Y	N	N/A	ACTION
	relationships with children and their families in the learning environment; b) personally review relationships to ensure that positive components of self-understanding are included and practiced, (e.g., openness, warmth) and negative components are excluded (e.g., power struggles, manipulation).				
11.1.3	Request a peer review to obtain feedback from colleagues about one's personal interactions and practices.				
11.1.4	Identify **Action Plan** related to one's requirements and follow through on implementation.				

11.2 Take opportunity for effective professional development.

	TASKS	Y	N	N/A	ACTION
11.2.1	Participate in educational programs to maintain up-to-date information/techniques/strategies therefore building continued competency.				
11.2.2	a) Exchange jobs with another staff member in the Center/School for a minimum of one week, or five days annually. b) Visit another day care/nursery school/kindergarten, Head Start, etc., two times per year with other educators. c) Be active in related professional organizations.				

Y = Yes   N = No   N/A = Not Applicable

The Early Childhood Educator will demonstrate a commitment to the education and care of young children through Knowledge, Interaction, and Communication in partnership with the family.

I Will:

11.	Establish positive relationships, focusing on a comprehensive system of communication with Colleagues.

11.3 Support and encourage one another in the role.

	TASKS	Y	N	N/A	ACTION
11.3.1	Contribute to a newsletter issued to all staff twice annually.				
11.3.2	Meet with Program team members weekly.				
11.3.3	Take an active role in center-planned events.				
11.3.4	Request observation and feed-back from a colleague on a monthly basis.				
11.3.5	Upon invitation, observe a different program 30 minutes each month. Share recorded observation/feedback with observed program.				
11.3.6	Identify problems as they arise. *Ex. Observer "Help me to understand what you intended ..."*				

11.4 Schedule meetings with colleagues regularly or as needed.

	TASKS	Y	N	N/A	ACTION
11.4.1	Attend weekly staff meetings.				
11.4.2	Demonstrate effective problem solving as needed.				
11.4.3	Meet with supervisor/principal to discuss matters pertaining to the center/school.				

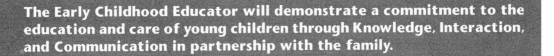

The Early Childhood Educator will demonstrate a commitment to the education and care of young children through Knowledge, Interaction, and Communication in partnership with the family.

11.	Establish positive relationships, focusing on a comprehensive system of communication with Colleagues.

11.5 Schedule opportunities to discuss current and established Early Childhood Education practices.

	TASKS	Y	N	N/A	ACTION
11.5.1	Attend meetings with other staff to discuss new information relevant to the field.				
11.5.2	Attend meetings to resolve issues/discuss policies.				

11.6 Demonstrate awareness of all operating policies.

	TASKS	Y	N	N/A	ACTION
11.6.1	Review all policies on an annual basis and be prepared to state them when asked.				
11.6.2	Review appropriate licensing regulations to ensure compliance with recommended regulations.				
11.6.3	Review and understand policies pertaining to child abuse.				

11.7 Demonstrate involvement in community/provincial/state Early Childhood Education-related professional associations.

	TASKS	Y	N	N/A	ACTION
11.7.1	Become a member of the professional associations.				
11.7.2	Become **involved** in profession-related organizations.				

Y = Yes   N = No   N/A = Not Applicable

The Early Childhood Educator will demonstrate a commitment to the education and care of young children through Knowledge, Interaction, and Communication in partnership with the family.

I Will:

12. Establish positive relationships, focusing on a comprehensive system of communication with the Community.

12.1 Network with other child-related agencies as required.

	TASKS	Y	N	N/A	ACTION
12.1.1	Participate in planning for an outside agency to address families on a particular topic. *Ex. Child Guidance.*				
12.1.2	Meet with necessary agencies/ boards in information sharing/ advocacy role for children with special needs.				
12.1.3	Actively initiate linkages with child care and health consultants to facilitate the concept of a seamless day.				

12.2 Participate in relevant projects or committees in the Community.

	TASKS	Y	N	N/A	ACTION
12.2.1	Take part in child-related events in the Community.				
12.2.2	Participate on other community child-related boards. *Ex. Child care/teacher groups.*				

12.3 Promote quality child care within the Community.

	TASKS	F	O	S	ACTION
12.3.1	Demonstrate courtesy, both written and verbal, to visitors and telephone callers.				
12.3.2	Plan and promote on-site events that include the community.				

Y = Yes   N = No   N/A = Not Applicable   F = Frequently   O = Occasionally   S = Seldom

SECTION II:

Curriculum: Review, Development, Implementation

DEMONSTRATED BEHAVIORS

 The Early Childhood Educator will demonstrate a commitment to the Review, Development, and Implementation of curriculum with a focus on play and experiential learning.

I Will:

1. Facilitate effective planning reflecting the observed developmental needs of all children.

2. Facilitate the emergence of knowledge and skills in each of the following domains:

2.1 COGNITIVE DOMAIN:

2.1.1 Promote spontaneity, curiosity, and discovery learning, indoors and outdoors.

2.1.2 Plan experiences to encourage the child to initiate self-directed learning experiences.

2.1.3 Provide a range of opportunities for children to explore and demonstrate critical thinking, problem solving, and reasoning skills.

2.1.4 Provide a range of opportunities for children to explore construction and manipulation of the environment through appropriate play experiences.

2.1.5 Promote an understanding of early mathematics.

2.1.6 Promote an understanding of early science concepts.

2.1.7 Promote an understanding of technological pursuits as they apply to the child's world.

2.2 AESTHETIC/CREATIVE DOMAIN:

2.2.1 Establish a climate for the child to explore, enjoy, and develop competence in the arts using a range of materials (see Section III).

2.2.2 Promote the use of equipment in a variety of ways.

2.2.3 Promote dramatic play to encourage fantasy, imitation, role playing, and dramatizing.

2.2.4 Promote an appreciation of beauty in nature and the arts.

2.3 AFFECTIVE DOMAIN:

2.3.1 Promote feelings of confidence and self-worth.

2.4 LANGUAGE/LITERACY DOMAIN:

2.4.1 Sustain and extend a positive attitude toward the development and use of language, both receptive and expressive, as a vehicle for learning.

2.4.2 Provide an opportunity for the development of early writing skills.

2.4.3 Provide an opportunity for children to develop early reading skills.

2.4.4 Provide appropriate language models and verbal interactions.

2.5 SOCIAL DOMAIN:

2.5.1 Establish a climate in which children can learn aspects of social skills development and experience healthy social interactions.

2.5.2 Promote a socially competent pro-social environment reflecting respect, kindness, and compassion for others.

2.6 PHYSICAL DOMAIN:

2.6.1 Promote health and safety requirements.

2.6.2 Promote appropriate nutrition requirements.

2.6.3 Promote fine and gross motor skills both indoors and outdoors.

3. Review child's progress in relation to the developmental continuum and individual goals.

   3.1 Evaluate program activities weekly/monthly.

   3.2 Use observation to review the emphasis in curriculum areas as well as goals for the individual child.

CHECKLIST

✳	**The Early Childhood Educator will demonstrate a commitment to the Review, Development, and Implementation of curriculum with a focus on play and experiential learning.**

I Will:

1. **Facilitate effective planning reflecting the observed developmental needs of all children.**

TASKS	Y	N	N/A	ACTION
1.1 Review developmental charts to ensure appropriate planning for each age group. (APPENDIX B)				
1.2 Plan developmental objectives for each group/child defining physical, language, cognitive, affective, social, and aesthetic goals.				
1.3 Use an effective, well-established planning technique to incorporate developmental objectives with the learning focus and child's interest. *Ex. Curriculum Webs* (APPENDIX E).				
1.3.1 Use a planning sheet to develop a weekly plan with criteria for planning appropriate programming objectives for infant, toddler, preschool, school-aged, and multiaged groupings. (APPENDIX E)				
1.4 a) Provide time for creative expression with a balance between playtime/routine time. b) Promote flexibility. c) Promote a balance of child-initiated and teacher-initiated experiences. d) Act upon child's interests/ needs and requests.				
1.5 Plan for solitary play.				
1.6 Plan for transitions from one activity to another.				
1.7 Plan outdoor play experiences on a daily basis.				

Y = Yes   N = No   N/A = Not Applicable

The Early Childhood Educator will demonstrate a commitment to the Review, Development, and Implementation of curriculum with a focus on play and experiential learning.

I Will:

2. Facilitate the emergence of knowledge and skills in each of the following domains:

2.1 **COGNITIVE DOMAIN:**

2.1.1 **Promote spontaneity, curiosity, and discovery learning, indoors and outdoors.**

TASKS	Y	N	N/A	ACTION
2.1.1.1 Utilize open-ended materials that promote discovery learning and purposeful investigative generation of ideas.				
2.1.1.2 Plan specific science areas or experiences that encourage curiosity and discovery learning.				
2.1.1.3 Include ideas to be shared and expanded.				
2.1.1.4 Include a Discovery Learning Center[1] once each month through preparation/sharing.				
[1] *Discovery Learning Center: A small, eye-catching, highly visual area set up in a playroom to emphasize a specific interest. The subject of the Discovery Center can either be initiated by the children or in support of the current theme.*				

2.1.2 **Plan experiences to encourage the child to actively initiate self-directed learning experiences.**

TASKS	F	O	S	ACTION
2.1.2.1 Introduce a wide variety of material to promote a spirit of inquiry.				
2.1.2.2 Introduce self-correcting activities.				
2.1.2.3 Promote decision-making— the power to choose. *Ex. "Of all the activities planned today, which one would you like to do first?"*				

(continued)

Y = Yes   N = No   N/A = Not Applicable   F = Frequently   O = Occasionally   S = Seldom

The Early Childhood Educator will demonstrate a commitment to the Review, Development, and Implementation of curriculum with a focus on play and experiential learning.

Facilitate the emergence of knowledge and skills in the COGNITIVE DOMAIN.

2.1.2 Plan experiences to encourage the child to actively initiate self-directed learning experiences *(continued)*

TASKS	F	O	S	ACTION
2.1.2.4 Encourage children to problem-solve and to produce more than one solution to a problem. *Ex. Amy is sorting a box of crayons/pencils/markers. "How else could you sort these? Is there another way?"*				
2.1.2.5 Provide a range of opportunities for children to explore thinking and reasoning skills through play activities. a) Sand/water b) Cooking/baking experiences c) Natural/physical science d) Manipulative materials e) Block play f) Wood working experiences g) Numeracy experiences h) Literal experiences				

2.1.3 Provide a range of opportunities for children to explore and demonstrate critical thinking and reasoning skills.

TASKS	F	O	S	ACTION
2.1.3.1 Develop and refine investigative skills. *Ex. "Where do you think the ant is going with that little piece of food?"*				
2.1.3.2 Prepare the environment to support planning, decision-making, and reflection by child. *Ex. "Let's get a magnifying glass and follow it."*				

F = Frequently   O = Occasionally   S = Seldom

The Early Childhood Educator will demonstrate a commitment to the Review, Development, and Implementation of curriculum with a focus on play and experiential learning.

I Will:

Facilitate the emergence of knowledge and skills in the COGNITIVE DOMAIN.

2.1.4 Provide a range of opportunities for children to explore construction and manipulation of the environment through appropriate play experiences.

TASKS	F	O	S	ACTION
2.1.4.1 Play experiences with unit blocks.				
2.1.4.2 Play experiences with board games.				
2.1.4.3 Play experiences with puzzles.				
2.1.4.4 Three-dimensional construction materials—e.g., duplo, lego, construx.				

2.1.5 Promote an understanding of early mathematics.

TASKS	F	O	S	ACTION
2.1.5.1 Demonstrate an understanding of number sense and numeration. *Ex. Sorting, classifying, and matching.*				
2.1.5.2 Demonstrate an understanding of measurement. *Ex. Ordering, weighing, measuring, cooking.*				
2.1.5.3 Demonstrate an understanding of spatial sense and geometry. *Ex. Accurate language: Use language accuracy, above, below, beside, i.e., sort three-dimensional objects like balls.*				
2.1.5.4 Demonstrate an understanding of patterning. *Ex. Red blocks alternating with blue blocks.*				

The Early Childhood Educator will demonstrate a commitment to the Review, Development, and Implementation of curriculum with a focus on play and experiential learning.

Facilitate the emergence of knowledge and skills in the COGNITIVE DOMAIN

2.1.5 Promote an understanding of early mathematics. *(continued)*

TASKS	F	O	S	ACTION
2.1.5.5 Demonstrate an understanding of data management and probability. *Ex. Sort items using color or other characteristics and create a graph.* *Ex. Use language of probability such as chance, luck, might.*				

2.1.6 Promote an understanding of early science concepts.

TASKS	F	O	S	ACTION
2.1.6.1 Plan for exploration and experimentation. *Ex. Request the child to describe a natural occurrence using his or her own observation, e.g., sprouting seeds, falling leaves.* *Ex. Observe and discuss characteristics of natural materials and demonstrate understanding of some basic concepts related to them.* *Ex. Highlight and describe with the child the function of common objects found at home and at school, i.e., tools, cooking utensils, toys.*				

2.1.7 Promote an understanding of technological pursuits as they apply to the child's world.

TASKS	F	O	S	ACTION
2.1.7.1 Use familiar technology appropriately. *Ex. Overhead projectors, cassette recorders, computers.*				
2.1.7.2 Identify familiar technological items and describe their use in daily life. *Ex. Telephone, videocassette recorder.*				

F = Frequently   O = Occasionally   S = Seldom

(continued)

The Early Childhood Educator will demonstrate a commitment to the Review, Development, and Implementation of curriculum with a focus on play and experiential learning.

I Will:

Facilitate the emergence of knowledge and skills in the COGNITIVE DOMAIN.

2.1.7 Promote an understanding of technological pursuits as they apply to the child's world. *(continued)*

TASKS	F	O	S	ACTION
2.1.7.3 Make things, using a variety of tools and techniques. *Ex. Hammer, screwdriver, glue, stapler.*				
2.1.7.4 Work with others in using technology. *Ex. Share tools, build as a group; work in pairs at the computer.*				
2.1.7.5 Demonstrate awareness that familiar objects are designed to suit the human body. *Ex. Mittens and gloves, tricycles.*				

2.2 AESTHETIC/CREATIVE DOMAIN:

2.2.1 Establish a climate for children to explore, enjoy, and develop competence in the arts using a range of materials (see Section III).

TASKS	F	O	S	ACTION
2.2.1.1 Explore various mediums and provide for the development of competence in an art experience. *Ex.* 1) *Mix paint to create new colors and textures;* 2) *Use familiar materials in a new way.*				
2.2.1.2 Explore choices and provide for the development of competence in a music experience. *Ex. Use finger plays, rhymes, and creative movement to music.*				

> **The Early Childhood Educator will demonstrate a commitment to the Review, Development, and Implementation of curriculum with a focus on play and experiential learning.**

Facilitate the emergence of knowledge and skills in the AESTHETIC/COGNITIVE DOMAIN.

2.2.2   Promote the use of equipment in a variety of ways.

TASKS	F	O	S	ACTION
2.2.2.1 In block play.				
2.2.2.2 In sand play.				
2.2.2.3 In dramatic play. *Ex. Blanket used as a tent.*				

2.2.3   Promote dramatic play to encourage fantasy, imitation, role playing, and dramatizing.

TASKS	F	O	S	ACTION
2.2.3.1 Plan settings and prepare materials for dramatic play. *Ex. Play house/doctor's office/ restaurant/hairdresser.*				

2.2.4   Promote an appreciation of beauty in nature and the arts.

TASKS	F	O	S	ACTION
2.2.4.1 Display a small collection of art work at child's level. Ask an open-ended question. *Ex. Teacher: "Which pictures did you like best? Why?"*				

2.3   **AFFECTIVE DOMAIN:**

2.3.1 Promote feelings of confidence and self-worth.

TASKS	F	O	S	ACTION
2.3.1.1 Ensure that the child has adequate information to learn a new skill.				
2.3.1.2 Encourage the child to reflect on successes. *Ex. Teacher: "How did you feel when you climbed up on that high climber?"*				

(continued)

F = Frequently   O = Occasionally   S = Seldom

The Early Childhood Educator will demonstrate a commitment to the Review, Development, and Implementation of curriculum with a focus on play and experiential learning.

I Will:

Facilitate the emergence of knowledge and skills in the AFFECTIVE DOMAIN.

2.3.1   Promote feelings of confidence and self-worth. *(continued)*

TASKS		F	O	S	ACTION
2.3.1.3	Provide new and unique experiences on a daily basis.				
2.3.1.4	Encourage self-help skills. *Ex. "Teresa, you can pour your own juice from the pitcher."*				
2.3.1.5	Give the child appropriate levels of responsibility. *Ex. Four-year-old Jonathon puts the napkins on the table for lunch.*				
2.3.1.6	Empower children to value themselves, others, ideas, and things. *Ex. "Hi Tony! Glad you could be here! Would you like to see what Andy brought to school today?"*				
2.3.1.7	Greet children so that they feel welcome. *Ex. As Sarah and her mother came into the room, I said, "Good Morning, Sarah. It's so nice to see you this morning."*				
2.3.1.8	Plan activities to promote self- knowledge. *Ex. Body tracing, face painting.*				
2.3.1.9	Plan for self awareness in daily events. *Ex. Teacher asks "Who has brown eyes?"*				
2.3.1.10	Ensure that the child has something personal in the program. *Ex. a) Show and Tell. b) Family picture.*				

(continued)

F = Frequently   O = Occasionally   S = Seldom

The Early Childhood Educator will demonstrate a commitment to the Review, Development, and Implementation of curriculum with a focus on play and experiential learning.

Facilitate the emergence of knowledge and skills in the AFFECTIVE DOMAIN.

2.3.1   Promote feelings of confidence and self-worth. *(continued)*

TASKS	F	O	S	ACTION
2.3.1.11 Promote conversation that will help a child understand the effect they have on another. ***Ex.*** *"Dominique liked the way you helped her with the puzzle."*				
2.3.1.12 Provide opportunities for the child to express emotion. ***Ex.*** *"You are very angry with Sam. You can tell him that."*				

2.4   LANGUAGE/LITERACY DOMAIN:

2.4.1   Sustain and extend a positive attitude toward the development and use of language, both receptive and expressive, as a vehicle for learning.

TASKS	F	O	S	ACTION
2.4.1.1 Provide opportunities for self-expression throughout the day. ***Ex.*** *When singing, "If You're Happy and You Know It," the teacher asks the children what they do when they are happy/sad/angry, etc.*				
2.4.1.2 Provide opportunities for imitation and modeling of language and sounds. ***Ex.*** *a) Sound of animals.* *b) Correct use of language/ grammar.* *c) Other languages.* *d) Sign language.*				
2.4.1.3 Be in tune with a child's need to express personal interests. ***Ex.*** *"Tell me about your Grandma's visit."*				

(continued)

F = Frequently   O = Occasionally   S = Seldom

The Early Childhood Educator will demonstrate a commitment to the Review, Development, and Implementation of curriculum with a focus on play and experiential learning.

I Will:

Facilitate the emergence of knowledge and skills in the LANGUAGE/LITERACY DOMAIN.

2.4.1 Sustain and extend a positive attitude toward the development and use of language, both receptive and expressive, as a vehicle for learning. *(continued)*

TASKS	F	O	S	ACTION
2.4.1.4 Recognize and respond to children's humor. *Ex. "That was a funny joke you just told. Would you like to tell John now?"*				
2.4.1.5 Facilitate a variety of experiences that promote language development in a positive and joyful way. *Ex. Story telling, puppetry, drama.*				
2.4.1.6 Follow child's lead during conversation. *Ex. Joey says, "I don't think this is the right way to play this game." Teacher responds, "How do you think it should be played?"*				
2.4.1.7 Encourage conversations by asking open-ended questions. *Ex. "Why do you think John is angry?"*				
2.4.1.8 Promote awareness of the connection between oral and written language. *Ex. a) Environmental print signs such as stop/ exit signs. b) Stories dictated by child.*				
2.4.1.9 Provide opportunities for listening to language in its whole form to ensure that children appreciate the communication function of written language. *Ex. Reading stories, poems, etc.*				

F = Frequently   O = Occasionally   S = Seldom

The Early Childhood Educator will demonstrate a commitment to the Review, Development, and Implementation of curriculum with a focus on play and experiential learning.

Facilitate the emergence of knowledge and skills in the LANGUAGE/LITERACY DOMAIN.

2.4.2 Provide opportunities for the development of early writing skills.

TASKS	F	O	S	ACTION
2.4.2.1 Demonstrate the connection between oral and written language. *Ex. The teacher says while writing a letter to thank a special visitor, "I'm writing what I am saying."*				
2.4.2.2 Demonstrate that writing communicates a message. *Ex. Environmental print: enter/exit; open/closed).*				
2.4.2.3 Encourage children to experiment with writing (a writing center).				
2.4.2.4 Model writing every day.				

2.4.3 Provide opportunities for children to develop early reading skills.

TASKS	F	O	S	ACTION
2.4.3.1 Encourage listening to stories, poems, and nonfiction materials for enjoyment and information.				
2.4.3.2 Request an appropriate response to a variety of materials read aloud. *Ex. Frequently told stories.*				
2.4.3.3 Ask the child to identify a favorite book and retell the story in his or her own words.				
2.4.3.4 Ask children to make predictions. *Ex. Anticipating what might come next.*				

(continued)

F = Frequently   O = Occasionally   S = Seldom

The Early Childhood Educator will demonstrate a commitment to the Review, Development, and Implementation of curriculum with a focus on play and experiential learning.

I Will:

Facilitate the emergence of knowledge and skills in the LANGUAGE/LITERACY DOMAIN.

2.4.3   **Provide opportunities for children to develop early reading skills.** *(continued)*

	TASKS	F	O	S	ACTION
2.4.3.5	Provide opportunities for children to make connections between their own experiences and those of storybook characters.				
2.4.3.6	Discuss some conventions of written materials. *Ex. Text written from left to right and words spelled with upper- and lowercase letters*				
2.4.3.7	Discuss features of books and other written material. *Ex. Title/illustrations. Use these features to help them understand the printed text. Also tell the story by looking at the pictures.*				
2.4.3.8	Explore letters of the alphabet and demonstrate understanding that letters represent sounds and written word conveys meaning. *Ex. Environmental print or short labels.*				
2.4.3.9	Use sound patterns to identify and predict words. *Ex. Rhymes and finger plays.*				
2.4.3.10	Provide continuing experiences recognizing, printing, and identifying letters in his or her name where the child shows readiness.				

F = Frequently   O = Occasionally   S = Seldom

The Early Childhood Educator will demonstrate a commitment to the Review, Development, and Implementation of curriculum with a focus on play and experiential learning.

Facilitate the emergence of knowledge and skills in the LANGUAGE/LITERACY DOMAIN.

2.4.4   Provide appropriate language models and verbal interactions.

TASKS	F	O	S	ACTION
2.4.4.1 Teacher demonstrates appropriate word choice. *Ex. Avoid slang; e.g., "you guys"; "kids."*				
2.4.4.2 Plan for and recognize the wide range of language differences in children.				

2.5   **SOCIAL DOMAIN:**

2.5.1   **Establish a climate in which children can learn aspects of social skills development and experience healthy social interactions.**

TASKS	F	O	S	ACTION
2.5.1.1 Encourage children to express appreciation of each other's special skills and contributions to the group. *Ex. "John, we enjoyed your story. Thank you for sharing it with us."*				
2.5.1.2 Model and encourage social competency that includes trust in others and self-responsibility. *Ex. Teacher asks, "Ann, you sound upset. What would you like to do about that?"*				
2.5.1.3 Model friendly, pleasant language that promotes cordial interactions.				
2.5.1.4 Demonstrate strategies leading to cooperative exchanges. *Ex. Teacher says "I'd like to hear about your toy, Assunta."*				
2.5.1.5 Encourage positive problem-solving skills to resolve conflicts. *Ex. Active listening; "I" messages.*				

F = Frequently   O = Occasionally   S = Seldom

The Early Childhood Educator will demonstrate a commitment to the Review, Development, and Implementation of curriculum with a focus on play and experiential learning.

I Will:

Facilitate the emergence of knowledge and skills in the SOCIAL DOMAIN.

2.5.2   Promote a socially competent pro-social environment reflecting respect, kindness, and compassion for others.

TASKS	F	O	S	ACTION
2.5.2.1 Model respect, cooperation, sharing, problem-solving with parents, children, and staff.				
2.5.2.2 Model a sense of humor.				
2.5.2.3 Incorporate appreciation of ethnic origins by celebrating customs of other countries.				
2.5.2.4 Encourage equity and inclusion by using the diversity, anti-bias checklist. (APPENDIX F)				
2.5.2.5 Provide opportunities for interaction with individuals of diverse abilities, ages, and gender.				
2.5.2.6 Model a pro-active approach when exclusion/prejudice is shown. *Ex. Child: "Why is Ryan in a wheelchair?" Teacher: "That's how he gets from one place to another. Would you like to try his wheelchair?"*				

2.6   **PHYSICAL DOMAIN**

2.6.1   **Promote health and safety requirements.**

TASKS	F	O	S	ACTION
2.6.1.1 Use proper sanitary practices. *Ex. Engage in an appropriate hand and toy washing procedure according to approved policy.*				

(continued)

F = Frequently   O = Occasionally   S = Seldom

The Early Childhood Educator will demonstrate a commitment to the Review, Development, and Implementation of curriculum with a focus on play and experiential learning.

Facilitate the emergence of knowledge and skills in the PHYSICAL DOMAIN.

2.6.1 Promote health and safety requirements. *(continued)*

	TASKS	F	O	S	ACTION
2.6.1.2	Follow policy to practice control of communicable disease.				
2.6.1.3	Each program will complete a safety checklist four times per year as the seasons change. (APPENDIX G)				
2.6.1.4	Each program staff will ensure daily maintenance of their area.				
2.6.1.5	Post a quick reference to First Aid.				
2.6.1.6	Check First Aid kits monthly and ensure notification if incomplete. Bandages will be checked monthly and replenished when needed.				
2.6.1.7	Keep current First Aid and Infant C.P.R. practices.				
2.6.1.8	Ensure ice, snow, water, and garbage removal as required.				
2.6.1.9	Plan for rest appropriate to the child's needs.				
2.6.1.10	Ensure that the family is aware of *any* illness or accident to their child.				
2.6.1.11	Ensure that the family is aware of any infectious disease that is affecting any child in the program.				
2.6.1.12	Ensure that the family is aware of contagious diseases in the Center.				

F = Frequently   O = Occasionally   S = Seldom

The Early Childhood Educator will demonstrate a commitment to the Review, Development, and Implementation of curriculum with a focus on play and experiential learning.

I Will:

Facilitate the emergence of knowledge and skills in the PHYSICAL DOMAIN.

2.6.2   Promote appropriate nutrition requirements.

TASKS	F	O	S	ACTION
2.6.2.1 Observe revised approved Food Guide by using a checklist.				
2.6.2.2 Post allergies.				
2.6.2.3 Children will be actively involved in preparing snacks.				
2.6.2.4 Meals to include items of high nutritional value. *Ex. Brown bread, brown rice, etc.*				
2.6.2.5 Arrange for attractive food presentation.				
2.6.2.6 Ensure that the child's nutritional needs are consistent with parental expectations.				
2.6.2.7 Observe ethnic requirements. *Ex. Jewish dietary rules.*				
2.6.2.8 Encourage meal exposure to various ethnic foods.				

2.6.3   Promote fine and gross motor skills both indoor and outdoors.

TASKS	F	O	S	ACTION
2.6.3.1 Using an inviting presentation, motivate the child to be involved with fine motor skills daily. *Ex. Stringing, cutting, painting.*				
2.6.3.2 Using an inviting presentation, motivate the child to be involved with large motor skills daily, indoors and/or outdoors. *Ex. Jumping, skipping, running.*				

F = Frequently   O = Occasionally   S = Seldom

(continued)

The Early Childhood Educator will demonstrate a commitment to the Review, Development, and Implementation of curriculum with a focus on play and experiential learning.

Facilitate the emergence of knowledge and skills in the PHYSICAL DOMAIN.

2.6.3 Promote fine and gross motor skills both indoor and outdoors. *(continued)*

TASKS	F	O	S	ACTION
2.6.3.3 Provide a demonstration of skills and techniques for children to model. *Ex. Gluing, holding scissors, holding brush*				

3. Review child's progress in relation to the developmental continuum and individual goals.

3.1 Evaluate program activities weekly/monthly.

TASKS	F	O	S	ACTION
3.1.1 A weekly checklist is used by each program as a method of evaluating group goals and monitoring change. (APPENDIX H)				
3.1.2 Monitor program reflecting long-term individual goals based on developmental outcomes monthly. (APPENDICES B and E)				

3.2 Use observation to review the emphasis in curriculum areas as well as goals for the individual child.

TASKS	Y	N	N/A	ACTION
3.2.1 Observe and record children's interests and requests.				
3.2.2 Observe and record children's interaction and planned activities.				

Y = Yes   N = No   N/A = Not Applicable   F = Frequently   O = Occasionally   S = Seldom

SECTION III:

Preparing the Physical Environment

DEMONSTRATED BEHAVIORS

 The Early Childhood Educator will demonstrate a commitment to Preparing the Environment for Learning.

I Will:

1. Organize the physical setting to maximize the achievements of educational/developmental goals and needs of children.

2. Equip the space to provide diverse materials necessary for holistic learning to occur in all domains.

    2.1 Cognitive Domain

    2.2 Aesthetic/Creative Domain

    2.3 Affective Domain

    2.4 Language/Literacy Domain

    2.5 Social Domain

    2.6 Physical Domain

3. Maintain physical space to ensure children's growth and encourage respect for property.

4. Establish a Community focus that encourages inclusivity and partnerships.

CHECKLIST

The Early Childhood Educator will demonstrate a commitment to Preparing the Environment for Learning.

I Will:

1. Organize the physical setting to maximize the achievements of educational/developmental goals and needs of children.

TASKS	Y	N	N/A	ACTION
1.1 Provide for quiet and active play.				
1.2 Provide space for routine function to promote independence.				
1.3 Incorporate diverse aesthetic/homelike/nurturing characteristics using appropriate furnishings and decor.				
1.4 Ensure that the equipment is child size and appropriate (e.g., child's feet can touch floor).				
1.5 Maximize use of the natural environment.				
1.6 Provide for a child's need to be alone/to rest.				
1.7 Promote social exchange through the use of physical space.				
1.8 Exemplify a family focus by including multi-aged multi-generational experiences.				
1.9 Provide decor that has a welcoming atmosphere.				
1.10 Promote environmentally sensitive responsibilities. *Ex. Reduce, Reuse, Recycle.*				
1.11 Rotate/change materials on a weekly basis, or when children have demonstrated ability, to encourage mastery of new skills. *Ex. Lego® blocks or unit blocks encourage ongoing skill development. Puzzles and books can be changed more often.*				

(continued)

Y = Yes   N = No   N/A = Not Applicable

The Early Childhood Educator will demonstrate a commitment to Preparing the Environment for Learning.

1. **Organize the physical setting to maximize the achievements of educational/developmental goals and needs of children.** *(continued)*

TASKS	Y	N	N/A	ACTION
1.12 Promote space for child to explore.				
1.13 Ensure that the materials are accessible to children (e.g., can be reached without adult assistance).				
1.14 Make seasonal changes to environment.				

2. **Equip the space to provide materials necessary for holistic learning to occur in all domains.**

   Please Note: The following lists include materials **available** to a program. They may be shared with other programs.

2.1 COGNITIVE DOMAIN

INSTRUMENT	> 75%	50–75%	< 50%	ACTION
Measuring Tools: Ruler, tape measure, scales and weights, measuring cups and spoons, large liquid measuring units, calipers, thermometers, clock, stopwatch, calendar, hourglass or egg timer, counting rods.				
Equipment: Sand table, water table, computer and software, calculators, oven or hot plate, rock tumbler, aquarium and related equipment.				
Tools: Eye droppers, mortar and pestle, siphons, prisms, flashlight, compass, garden tools, screw, lamp, birdhouse, hoses, tongs, tweezers, locks and keys, stethoscope, weather vane.				
Simple machines: Screws, screwdriver, wheels, knives, pulleys, hammer, dowels, wheelbarrow, simple motors, battery with electric circuit setup, saw, windmill, waterwheel.				

(continued)

The Early Childhood Educator will demonstrate a commitment to Preparing the Environment for Learning.

2.1 COGNITIVE DOMAIN *(continued)*

INSTRUMENT	> 75%	50–75%	< 50%	ACTION
Sorting/Counting: (Multiple small objects that may be counted or grouped and that vary in size, shape, color, and type), abacus, counting rods, poker chips, Unifix cubes, collection of small objects, sorting mats.				
Signs and Symbols: Environmental print, e.g., stop/exit signs, numerals in sandpaper and written or other surfaces, traffic signals and signs, safety signs, labels as appropriate, math signs, pictographs of events or observations.				
Children's Literature: Picture books, nonfiction easy-to-read books, information books, atlas, dictionary, and big books.				
Literacy Materials: (1- and ½-inch) graph paper, notebooks, recipes, large paper for recording events, drawing materials/clipboard, hand signs, dual language books.				
Games: Board games, picture cards, games, standard playing cards, picture dominoes, lotto games, checkers, Chinese checkers, bingo-type games, pattern cards.				
Problem Solving: Objects of various attributes that sink and float, magnets (and objects that are or are not attracted to magnets), sorting boxes and materials that vary systematically by size, shape, texture, color, or function, pegboards and pegs, peg pattern card (magnets and prisms), color chips from paint stores, nuts and bolts, puzzles, sieves, funnels, containers of irregular size and				

(continued)

The Early Childhood Educator will demonstrate a commitment to Preparing the Environment for Learning.

2.1 COGNITIVE DOMAIN (continued)

INSTRUMENT	> 75%	50–75%	< 50%	ACTION
Problem Solving (continued): shape, Montessori graduated cylinders, unit blocks, nesting dolls or barrels.				
Living Things: Dish garden, plants, watering cans and fertilizer, plant containers, seeds of various sorts, potting soil, an animal (iguana, hamster, fish, snake, rabbit, turtle), appropriate cage(s) and food, litter, and cleaning supplies, ant farm, worm farm.				
Transportation Toys: Cars, trucks, boats, airplanes, trains and tracks, farm equipment, construction equipment.				
Materials from the Natural Environment: Leaves, stones, sticks or bark, grasses, grains, flowers, root systems, foods in the unprocessed state, insects.				
Models: Globe, maps, skeleton(s), plastic farm or wild animals, dinosaurs, insects, snakes, flowers, airplanes (realistic toys).				
Pictures: Photographs or drawings of objects or events that represent the physical or social environment related to units taught, films, filmstrips, videotapes.				
Blocks: Unit blocks, bristle blocks, cent-cubes snap blocks, large hollow blocks, foam and plastic blocks (cardboard or milk carton) unit cubes, small table blocks, Legos, various other blocks needed for math and science instruction.				

(continued)

The Early Childhood Educator will demonstrate a commitment to Preparing the Environment for Learning.

2.1 COGNITIVE DOMAIN (continued)

INSTRUMENT	> 75%	50–75%	< 50%	ACTION
Teacher Resources: Manuals for the use of science equipment, reference books on science, social studies, and other topics, reference books on math learning and teaching based on materials.				
Technological Equipment: Computer with appropriate programs.				
Construction Equipment: Wheeled storage for large blocks, large storage shelves for unit blocks, rug or carpet (crates, planks).				
Support Supplies: Carpet squares, tiles, and cloth pieces for rivers and roads, pulleys.				
Pictures Depicting: Other block structures, objects and events related to learning focus.				
Construction Sets: Knex®, Lincoln Logs®, various commercial sets.				
Art Supplies: See the list under "Aesthetic/ Creative Domain."				
Raw Materials: Water, sand clay, and dough (flour, salt, and alum), bee's wax.				
Woodworking: Workbench and vice, saw, hammer, nails, screws, sandpaper, bit and brace, screwdriver, level, carpenter's square, other woodworking equipment.				
Literacy Support Materials: Paper and pens for writing directions for constructing something, pictographs, letters and stories, easel stands, and pocket charts.				

The Early Childhood Educator will demonstrate a commitment to Preparing the Environment for Learning.

2.2 AESTHETIC/CREATIVE DOMAIN

INSTRUMENT	> 75%	50–75%	< 50%	ACTION
Equipment: Tape recorder/player (a separate children's tape player may be desirable for three- to five-year-olds), easel, woodworking bench or table with vice, table and chairs, open storage for art materials and supplies, camera, camcorder, head phones.				
Paper of Various Textures: Construction paper, tissue, glossy finger-paint paper, newsprint, cardboard, wallpaper, cellophane, standard reprocessed paper, sandpaper of different grains, waxed, contact paper, plates, small bags, tag board, plastic wrap, paper plates, tissues, papier-mâché strips, paper cups, rice paper.				
Paints, etc.: Watercolors, tempera, crayons, fingerpaint, ink, laundry starch to extend and thicken tempera, stamp pad and ink, items that naturally add color, e.g., grape juice, onion skins.				
Applicators: Flat and round brushes, tiny watercolor brushes, sponges, string, cotton swabs, feathers, paper cleaners, adult-type brushes, paste brushes, stamps with various designs, empty deodorant roll-on bottles, cotton balls.				
Drawing Instruments: Pencils, colored pencils, colored chalk, crayons, felt-tip pens, markers.				
Tools: Scissors, knives, flatware, kitchen tools, crewel needles, embroidery hoops, weaving frames, drinking straws, pails, water containers of				

(continued)

The Early Childhood Educator will demonstrate a commitment to Preparing the Environment for Learning.

2.2 AESTHETIC/CREATIVE DOMAIN *(continued)*

INSTRUMENT	> 75%	50–75%	< 50%	ACTION
Tools (continued): various sizes, lidded paint containers, muffin tin, source for heating, hole punch, grater, stapler, clay-working tools, toothbrushes, screening, rulers, pinking shears, rollers, cookie cutters, pie plates, cake tins.				
Sculpting Materials: Boxes, newspaper, papier-mâché strips, wire, wood pieces, potter's clay and storage container, Play-doh®, flour, alum, salt, cornstarch.				
Found Objects: Fabric scraps, netting, wood scraps, spools, paper tubes, small boxes, flat-surfaced stones, Popsicle® sticks, meat trays, egg or milk cartons, baby food jars, plastic bottles, Styrofoam® (nontoxic), paper pieces, feathers, egg shells, bottle caps.				
Adhesives: Paste, white glue, rubber cement, cellophane tape, masking tape, wallpaper paste, flour/water, egg white, gummed shapes or stickers.				
Cloth: Fabric scraps, net for embroidery thread, yarn, felt, pellon or other bonded inner lining (for story boards), lace, ribbon, rickrack.				
Prints: Paintings and reproductions of sculpture from around the world, well-illustrated children's books, photographs of nature, artwork, and musical instruments displayed in frames.				

(continued)

The Early Childhood Educator will demonstrate a commitment to Preparing the Environment for Learning.

2.2 AESTHETIC/CREATIVE DOMAIN *(continued)*

INSTRUMENT	> 75%	50–75%	< 50%	ACTION
Recordings: Music of all types, children's songs from around the world, excerpts from classical music for movement experiences, poetry.				
Instruments: Quality hand drum, rhythm instruments such as triangles, rhythm sticks, wood blocks, temple blocks, tambourines, cymbals, small and large drums, maracas, cleaves, piano, Autoharp, guitar, ukulele, melody bells, step bells, resonator bells, or tuning forks so that singing can start on pitch, real musical instruments borrowed or demonstrated as a part of the learning program.				
Literacy Support Materials: Easel or experience story stand and paper, heavy marker, music staff paper, children's books about art and artists and those involving music, paper and pencils, felt boards.				
Teacher Resources: Several song books for children including culturally diverse selections, one or more music series books, books on making instruments, musical games and movement activity books, books and recordings about instruments.				
Pretend Play Furniture: Doll bed, refrigerator, stove, sink, washer, chest of drawers, small coat rack, small table and chairs, rocking chair, child-sized sofa (if room exists), cabinets, mirror, clock radio, toaster, rug.				
Clothing: Dress-up clothes, hats for family, hats for community workers,				

(continued)

The Early Childhood Educator will demonstrate a commitment to Preparing the Environment for Learning.

2.2 AESTHETIC/CREATIVE DOMAIN *(continued)*

INSTRUMENT	> 75%	50–75%	< 50%	ACTION
Clothing (continued): aprons, laundry basket, clothesline, bedding for dolls, scarves, ribbons, shoes, vests, work boots, cloth strips for multiple purposes, curtains, turbans, kimonos, embroidered shirts, dasikis and dirndls, ceremonial dress, moccasins, beading.				
Dolls: Several dolls of various sizes and representing both sexes and different racial and cultural groups, doll clothes, washable stuffed animals, bottles, cradle, high chair, baby toys.				
Tools: Dishes, flatware, pots and pans, telephones, clothes baskets, ironing board and iron, cleaning equipment, suitcases, dishwashing supplies and equipment, woks, chopsticks, rice cookers, straw hats, crutches.				
Large Toys: Child-sized traffic signs, riding wheeled trucks, steering wheel mounted on a board, box or tree stump.				
Story Re-enactment: Props essential to retelling stories and simple costume props, folk tales and poems reflecting different cultures, abilities, and ages.				
Prop Boxes: Containers of necessary materials to promote play on a theme—e.g., hairdresser, doctor/nurse, etc.				
Other Materials: Extra props appropriate to specific learning focus (such as camping, spaceflight).				

The Early Childhood Educator will demonstrate a commitment to Preparing the Environment for Learning.

2.3 AFFECTIVE DOMAIN

INSTRUMENT	> 75%	50–75%	< 50%	ACTION
Equipment: Homelike furnishings, low room dividers (some with corkboard, some with holes and hooks), large pillows, child-sized easy chair, area rugs, cleaning equipment (child-sized broom, dustpan, carpet sweeper), lamp for private space, child-sized rocker, easy-access shelving and storage units, ethnic artwork and crafts.				
Cleaning Supplies: Dust cloths, sponges, pail, mop, spray bottles, pans.				
Children's Literature: Illustrated and non-illustrated books focusing on the emotional challenges of childhood such as new siblings, handling anger, accepting people who look or function differently, death, divorce, remarriage, bilingual labels, in Braille and sign language.				
Photographs: Depicting various emotions, people at work, ordinary people doing everyday tasks, people of various ages, races (ethnic origins as they are functioning in the United States and Canada today), cultural events or celebrations of a historical or traditional nature.				
Literacy Materials: Empty books for personal messages, personal telephone directories, personal calendars or schedules, tapes and tape recorders, drawing materials, paper, pencils.				

> ❋ **The Early Childhood Educator will demonstrate a commitment to Preparing the Environment for Learning.**

2.4 LANGUAGE/LITERACY DOMAIN

INSTRUMENT	> 75%	50–75%	< 50%	ACTION
Equipment: Listening center with headphones, tape recorder-player, audio filmstrip projector, videocassette recorder and television, (laminator, duplicator), computer and software, flannel board and easel, chalkboard, bulletin boards, book display shelving, storage units for equipment, big book easel, chart holder (adult-sized chair), telephones, computer printers.				
Paper: Lined and unlined, bound in empty books, small pads around the room, notebooks, tagboard strips, file cards, tagboards for charts, (laminating material), paper and holder for experience stories, chart paper, receipt or order pads, computer paper, newsprint, Post-it™ notes, all kinds of recording materials, tracing paper, flip chart.				
Writing Supplies: Thick and standard pencils, felt-tip pens, drawing or painting tools, stapler and staples, paper clips, gum erasers, adult- and child-sized scissors, tape dispenser, tape, stamps, envelopes.				
Charts and Pictures: Maps, graphs, charts illustrating instructional content and labeled, photographs, prints of paintings, charts displaying alphabet at child's-eye view (wherever they are needed or children are writing), work charts or classroom dictionaries related to topics of instruction, labels, written directions.				

(continued)

The Early Childhood Educator will demonstrate a commitment to Preparing the Environment for Learning.

2.4 LANGUAGE/LITERACY DOMAIN *(continued)*

INSTRUMENT	> 75%	50–75%	< 50%	ACTION
Audiovisual Materials: Commercially prepared tapes of children's books, films or videotapes of content and literature, teacher-made audiotapes of classroom books, flannelboard stories.				
Children's Literature: Illustrated and nonillustrated books and materials that are nonsexist and multicultural and reflect all aspects of diversity, focusing on: a) Fantasy b) Realism (i.e., emotionally challenging) c) Information d) Basic skills (i.e., shapes, numbers, letters)				
Literacy Support Materials: Word-based games, story sequence puzzles and games, selected software, finger puppets, child- sized puppets, large puppets, flannel board, flannel letters and numerals, letter templates, pocket charts.				

2.5 SOCIAL DOMAIN

INSTRUMENT	> 75%	50–75%	< 50%	ACTION
Material Requiring Cooperation: Long jump rope, games requiring two or more players, pretend telephones, hose or string and can phones, miniature transportation toys and signs.				
Play Props Supporting Social Play Themes: Small figures depicting age, race, and gender, small family dolls, community helper dolls, sets of small stores and houses on a street system, doll house with furnishings.				

(continued)

The Early Childhood Educator will demonstrate a commitment to Preparing the Environment for Learning.

2.5 SOCIAL DOMAIN (continued)

INSTRUMENT	> 75%	50–75%	< 50%	ACTION
Pictures: Photos and paintings such as sharing, helping, families, neighborhoods, clothing, occupations, historical events, stores of various kinds, nonsexist pictures.				
Play Props Supporting Diverse Cultures and Life Styles: Cooking equipment, clothing, pictures, and books from many races and social economic groups.				
Literacy Support Materials: Books selected to support common social experiences, camera and film for recording local community and school events, children's literature about family life and about families across the life cycle, paper supplies suitable for notes or tickets, pencils.				

2.6 PHYSICAL DOMAIN

INSTRUMENT	> 75%	50–75%	< 50%	ACTION
Balls: Sports, large rubber, Nerf®, small soft, marbles, beanbags, yarn.				
Tools: Bats, mallets, ping-pong paddles, Nerf® paddles, bowling pins, nets, baseball gloves, hoops, badminton set, snowshoes.				
Climbing and Balance: Balance beam, parallel bars, jungle gym, hung ropes, net climber, slide, planks and triangles, ladders, jump ropes.				
Wheeled Toys: Tricycles, pedal wheel toys and wagons (roller/ice skates, skateboards) scooter boards.				

(continued)

The Early Childhood Educator will demonstrate a commitment to Preparing the Environment for Learning.

2.6 PHYSICAL DOMAIN *(continued)*

INSTRUMENT	> 75%	50–75%	< 50%	ACTION
Manipulative Materials: Poultry baster, eyedropper, tongs of various types, tweezers, plastic or metal plumbing joints, beads, strings, plastic tubing, lacing boards, lacing shoe, button and zipper frame, computer mouse, Marble Run® or Plex-a-Plax® (or other more complicated "fit-together" materials with various commercial names), buttons with needles and thread.				
Food: Samples of foods from the basic food groups for children to learn to taste wide ranges of foods, foods prepared from various cultural groups, plastic models of foods.				
Health-related Supplies: Human thermometer, toothbrushes, toothpaste, paper cups, antiseptic soap, first aid kit, room thermometer, facial tissue, cleaning supplies, growth charts, sterile gloves, face masks.				
Music and Tapes: Dance audiotapes for children, music excerpts for free dance, musical game books and recordings, large drum.				
Literacy Support Materials: Sample menus from various cultures, children's recipes for healthy snacks, children's cookbooks, standard cookbooks.				
Additional Resources: Game collections including those requiring cooperation, games from various cultures (and ethnic groups), charts of the fundamental motor skills depicting increasing levels of maturity, small parachute.				

The Early Childhood Educator will demonstrate a commitment to Preparing the Environment for Learning.

I Will:

3. Maintain physical space to ensure children's growth and encourage respect for property.

TASKS	Y	N	N/A	ACTION
3.1 Ensure that repairs to equipment are reported to the appropriate source.				
3.2 Ensure that safety precautions are carried through. Assess environment indoor and outdoors for safety hazards on a regular basis.				
3.3 Report maintenance needs.				
3.4 Report the need for grounds maintenance.				
3.5 When possible, include the child when choosing and caring for equipment.				
3.6 Ensure a clean, well-organized environment (i.e., Educator will ensure that toys, equipment, and shelving are regularly cleaned and disinfected).				
3.7 Help children build respect for toys and equipment.				
3.8 Ensure that storage of materials promotes the use of find-use-return cycle.				

4. Establish a Community focus that encourages inclusivity and partnerships.

TASKS	Y	N	N/A	ACTION
4.1 Community bulletin boards reflecting events/activities of interest to the child and family.				
4.2 Plan and promote events that invite the Community to view quality child education and care.				

APPENDICES

Appendix A:
Foundation Principles of
Early Childhood Education

THE STEPS TO LIFELONG LEARNING

Our initial premise of basic Early Childhood Education philosophy is to acknowledge the value of a strong foundation to early learning. This basis would include several steps that, if accomplished with enduring quality, would strengthen one's ability to acquire the necessary skills for lifelong learning. The constitution of this foundation could be compared to a ladder or stairway where lifelong learning is at the top. This analogy continues in identifying the bottom and subsequent six steps to complete the theory.

The six main tasks (or steps) are:

◆ Trust
◆ Self-Value
◆ Self-Control
◆ Learning Tools
◆ Basic Skills
◆ Lifelong Learning

Lifelong learning is the final step. It is characterized by the desire and determination to go through all of these steps throughout the span of one's life.

The stages to lifelong learning are illustrated on the next page.

1. Trust

Developing trust in those around us is the basis of all our relationships. This starts in our postnatal state and continues through a lifetime. The need for trust reappears with every new relationship we form.

A child's first group experience is often the initial try at trusting adults other than the parent. Sensitive teachers make every effort to establish this necessary step by arranging visits to the home, getting to know the family, and drawing the experiences closer together.

Trust is based in security, protection without overprotection, and unconditional regard and acceptance.

With this firmly in place, we move onto the second "step" or level in the foundation of early learning.

2. Self-Value

Building a strong sense of self-identity strengthens the desire to belong to the group experience. Feeling valued and worthwhile increases self-confidence and as a result develops social skills.

STEPS IN THE FOUNDATION TO LIFELONG LEARNING

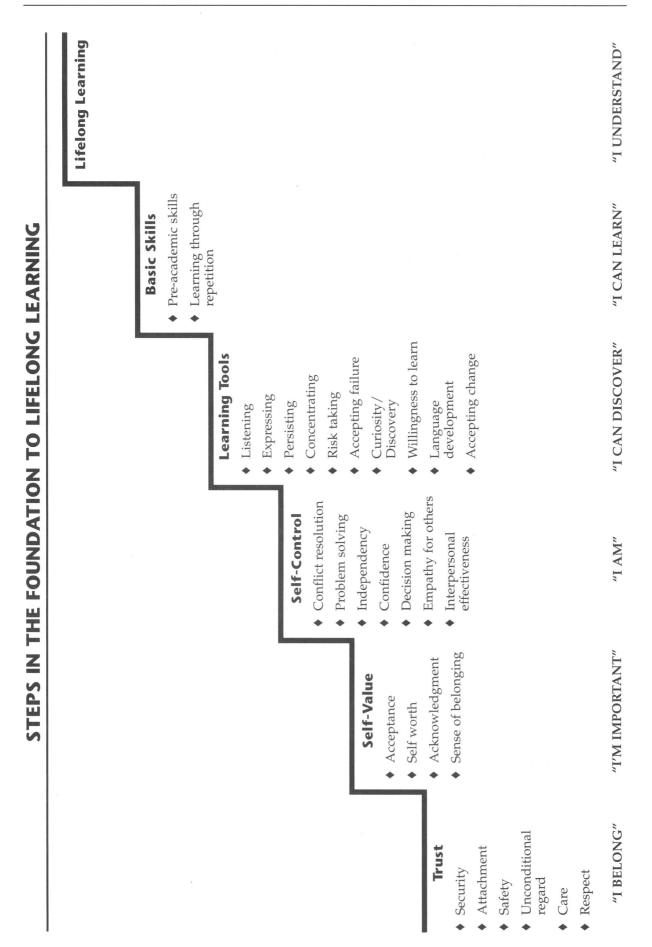

Lifelong Learning

"I UNDERSTAND"

Basic Skills
- ◆ Pre-academic skills
- ◆ Learning through repetition

"I CAN LEARN"

Learning Tools
- ◆ Listening
- ◆ Expressing
- ◆ Persisting
- ◆ Concentrating
- ◆ Risk taking
- ◆ Accepting failure
- ◆ Curiosity / Discovery
- ◆ Willingness to learn
- ◆ Language development
- ◆ Accepting change

"I CAN DISCOVER"

Self-Control
- ◆ Conflict resolution
- ◆ Problem solving
- ◆ Independency
- ◆ Confidence
- ◆ Decision making
- ◆ Empathy for others
- ◆ Interpersonal effectiveness

"I AM"

Self-Value
- ◆ Acceptance
- ◆ Self worth
- ◆ Acknowledgment
- ◆ Sense of belonging

"I'M IMPORTANT"

Trust
- ◆ Security
- ◆ Attachment
- ◆ Safety
- ◆ Unconditional regard
- ◆ Care
- ◆ Respect

"I BELONG"

How able are we to feel good about ourselves if our ability to trust others is impaired? Feeling positively about our self is a necessary step to facilitate pro-social behavior.

3. Self-Control

The third step in building the strong foundation of early experiences is to recognize our ability to control our own behavior—that is, we can make decisions that affect our behavior. The goal of this emotional control is our ability to discipline ourselves through intrinsic motivation as compared to extrinsic control. Assisting the child to problem-solve, adjust to social experiences, encourage independence, decision making, and cooperation enables the child to gain mastery in understanding emotional responses.

Controlling one's own emotions in a way that is satisfying to us is difficult in the absence of a positive self-image. Seeing oneself in a negative image leads to indecisive, often undesirable behavior.

4. Learning Tools

Our ability to feel accepted and secure, possess a strong self-value, ability to problem solve, and make decisions about our own behavior lends easy access to acquiring sound learning skills or learning tools. These dispositions facilitate the innate necessities to go on learning. We seldom learn these skills through drill and rote, yet they are essential to the satisfaction gained through learning. To develop an understanding of language, to be curious, to listen to others, to persist at a task until completed, to concentrate—all will help us learn. To share time and materials, to gain confidence, to comprehend meaning—all are useful in this process. To discover, to be inventive, to express ourselves, to be humorous, to be resourceful—all are skills necessary to the ambience of learning.

Learning occurs through relationships, hence a dependency on trust, self-identity, and self-discipline.

5. Basic Skills

Basic skills are the immediate forerunners to academic learning. Pre-reading, pre-math, and pre-printing provide us with the information required to read, compute, and write. These skills are learned as a result of consistency, rote, and drill. It is difficult to separate these units of actions from the disposition to learn as they seem to occur simultaneously. For example, you can learn the words to a song through repetition, but you cannot learn to like to sing in the same way. You can learn the words in a book, but wanting to read is different. Learning to write requires a love of written expression, which cannot be learned through repetitiously printing letters.

The attitudes and interests of the adults in a child's life charge the environment from which the modeling of learning skills or dispositions originates. This natural acquisition emanates from the relationships that have developed in the building of the foundation of early human experience. Through the vehicle of play, these avenues of learning are illuminated, strengthening social skills and language as voracious ingredients to the process.

6. Lifelong Learning

The cycle of these early childhood experiences can be reaffirmed throughout life. Academic educational opportunity is less complex, more successful, and satisfying with the strength of early education firmly in place.

If teachers and parents share this philosophy, the relationship existing between them is sustained.

Why Are These Steps So Important?

These steps are all interrelated, building on the step before. Each level of the ladder of learning must be completed with a certain amount of success. Children need to develop a sense of trust in order to develop relationships. To strengthen a sense of self-identity, an individual must feel valued, accepted, and worthwhile by others. This can only occur when trust has been established. Academic learning cannot take place successfully unless a child has acquired some learning tools and emotional control, which is difficult if self-esteem is low. Without listening skills, concentration, and self-discipline, academic learning becomes a struggle.

Early Childhood Educators, together with parents, can guide the young child through each step on the ladder of learning, beginning with trust and continuing with broadening of language and basic skills. At this last level, children should have the skills and confidence to advance to academic learning associated with formal education.

APPENDIX B:
Child Development
Chart and Checklist

The Child Development Chart begins on the next page. The Child Development Checklist begins on page 88.

Gross Motor Skills

0 to 12 Months	13 to 24 Months	25 to 36 Months	37 to 48 Months	49 to 60 Months	61 to 72 Months
◆ Lifts head and holds for 5 seconds while lying on stomach.	◆ Walks alone, at least three steps.	◆ Jumps in place, two feet together, and remains standing.	◆ Runs, changing directions.	◆ Walks backward toe-heel.	◆ Catches ball at distance of 5 feet.
◆ Holds head steady when held upright for at least 15 seconds while adult walks around.	◆ Pulls toy, pushes toy.	◆ Stands on one foot, with aid.	◆ Walks in a straight line.	◆ Jumps forward 10 times without falling.	◆ Walks on balance beam.
◆ Rolls from back to side.	◆ Walks without support for 10 feet without falling.	◆ Walks on tiptoe three steps.	◆ Balance on one foot for 5 to 10 seconds.	◆ Jumps over rope positioned at child's midcalf.	◆ Can cover 6½ feet (2 meters) hopping on one foot.
◆ Sits without support, without prompting.	◆ Moves from sitting to standing without support from object or person.		◆ Hops on one foot.	◆ Turns somersault.	◆ Skips on alternate feet.
◆ Crawls at least 2 feet alternating hands and feet while stomach is up off floor.	◆ Walks up and down stairs not alternating feet (hand held).		◆ Pushes, pulls, steers wheeled toys.		◆ Jumps rope.
◆ Pulls self to standing and stands unaided.	◆ Kicks ball forward without falling.		◆ Rides (steers and pedals) tricycle.		◆ Skates.
◆ Walks with aid.	◆ Moves to music.		◆ Uses slide without assistance.		
◆ Squats to pick up object and returns to standing without falling.	◆ Runs forward well.		◆ Jumps over 6-inch- (15 cm.) high object landing on both feet together.		
			◆ Throws ball overhand.		
			◆ Catches ball bounced to him or her.		
			◆ Walks up and down stairs alone alternating feet.		

Source: BRIGANCE® Diagnostic Inventory of Early Development. Copyright © 1991 Curriculum Associates®, Inc. Reprinted/Adapted by permission.

Fine Motor Skills

0 to 12 Months	13 to 24 Months	25 to 36 Months	37 to 48 Months	49 to 60 Months	61 to 72 Months
◆ Reaches, grasps, objects in mouth.	◆ Picks up things with thumb and index finger.	◆ Turns knobs.	◆ Uses one hand consistently.	◆ Cuts on line continuously.	◆ Cuts out simple shapes: triangle, circle, square.
◆ Picks things up with fingers against heel of palm (Palmer grasp).	◆ Builds tower of three small blocks.	◆ Strings large beads.	◆ Builds tower of nine small blocks.	◆ Copies cross.	◆ Copies first name.
◆ Transfers object from one hand to other hand.	◆ Puts four rings on stick.	◆ Turns pages singly of a primary book.	◆ Drives nails and pegs.	◆ Copies square.	◆ Prints numerals 1–5.
◆ Drops and picks up toy.	◆ Places five pegs in pegboard.	◆ Holds crayon with thumb and fingers, not fist.	◆ Copies circle.	◆ Prints a few capital letters.	◆ Colors within lines.
	◆ Turns pages two or three pages at a time.	◆ Uses one hand consistently in most activities.	◆ Manipulates clay materials (for example: rolls balls, snakes, cookies).		◆ Has handedness well established (that is, child is left- or right-handed).
	◆ Random scribbles without direction.	◆ Paints with some wrist actions, makes dots, lines, circular strokes.			◆ Pastes and glues appropriately.
	◆ Throws small ball at least 3 feet.	◆ Rolls, pounds, squeezes, and pulls clay.			
	◆ Paints with whole arm movement, shifts hands, makes strokes.	◆ Cuts paper in two with scissors.			

Source: BRIGANCE® *Diagnostic Inventory of Early Development.* Copyright © 1991 Curriculum Associates®, Inc. Reprinted/Adapted by permission.

Literacy/Expressive Language

0 to 12 Months	13 to 24 Months	25 to 36 Months	37 to 48 Months	49 to 60 Months	61 to 72 Months
◆ Makes crying and noncrying sounds.	◆ Says first meaningful word.	◆ Joins vocabulary words together in two-word phrases.	◆ Talks in sentences of three or more words, which take the form agent-action-location. *Ex. "Daddy, sit on chair."*	◆ Asks *when, how,* and *why* questions.	◆ Child engages in meaningful dialogue; *Ex. Gives and receives information.*
◆ Repeats some vowel and consonant sounds (babbles) when alone or when spoken to.	◆ Uses single words plus a gesture to indicate wants or needs.	◆ Gives first and last name.	◆ Tells about past experiences.	◆ Talks about causality by using *because* and *so.*	◆ Uses irregular past tense verbs; *Ex. I spoke; I drank.*
◆ Interacts with others by vocalizing after adult.	◆ Refers to self by name.	◆ Asks *what* and *where* questions.	◆ Uses *s* on nouns to indicate plurals.	◆ Tells the content of a story but may confuse facts.	◆ Communicates his/her feelings.
◆ Communicates meaning through intonation; *Ex. sound is more distinct.*	◆ Uses *my* and *mine* to indicate possession.	◆ Makes negative statements; *Ex. Can't open it.*	◆ Uses *ed* on verbs to indicate past tense.		
◆ Attempts to imitate speech sounds; *Ex. bye-bye.*	◆ Says successive words to describe an event.	◆ Shows frustration at not being understood.	◆ Repeats at least one nursery rhyme and can sing a song.		
	◆ Has vocabulary of about 20 words for people and common objects.		◆ Speech is understandable to strangers, but there is still some sound error.		

Source: BRIGANCE® Diagnostic Inventory of Early Development. Copyright © 1991 Curriculum Associates®, Inc. Reprinted/Adapted by permission.

Literacy/Receptive Language

0 to 12 Months	13 to 24 Months	25 to 36 Months	37 to 48 Months	49 to 60 Months	61 to 72 Months
◆ Responds to speech by looking at speaker.	◆ Understands simple phrases; *Ex. "Open the door," "Get the ball."*	◆ Can identify objects when told their use; *Ex. "Show me the one you brush your teeth with."*	◆ Understands size comparisons such as *big* and *bigger*.	◆ Understands comparatives like *big, bigger, biggest*.	◆ Recalls events from story presented orally without pictures.
◆ Responds differently to aspects of speaker's voice; *Ex. friendly or unfriendly, male or female.*	◆ Responds verbally or non-verbally when asked *where* when question is accompanied by gesture. *Ex. "Where is the dog?"*	◆ Understands question forms *what* and *where*.	◆ Understands relationships expressed by *if ..., then* or *because* sentences.	◆ Understands the use of plurals; *Ex. "Bring me the books."*	◆ Follows three unrelated directions; *Ex. Put the cup in the sink; Pick up the ball; Sit on the couch.*
◆ Turns to source of sound.	◆ Understands prepositions *on, in, under.*	◆ Understands negatives—*no, not, can't, don't.*	◆ Carries out a series of two to four related directions.	◆ Understands sequencing of events when told them; *Ex. "First we have to go to the store, then we can make the cake, and tomorrow we will eat it."*	
◆ Responds with gesture to *hi, bye-bye,* and *up* when these words are accompanied by appropriate gesture and tone.	◆ Follows request to bring familiar object from another room.	◆ Enjoys listening to simple story-books and requests them again.	◆ Understands when told "Let's pretend."		
	◆ Follows a series of two simple, but related directions.				

Cognitive Skills

0 to 12 Months	13 to 24 Months	25 to 36 Months	37 to 48 Months	49 to 60 Months	61 to 72 Months
◆ Child shows awareness of new situations; *Ex. showing surprise.*	◆ Imitates actions and words of adults.	◆ Responds to simple directions; *Ex. "Give me the ball and block." "Get your shoes and socks."*	◆ Recognizes and matches six colors.	◆ Plays with words; creates own rhyming words; says or makes words having similar sounds.	◆ Selects single word from visual presentation.
◆ Responds to strangers by crying or staring.	◆ Responds to words or commands with appropriate actions; *Ex. "Give me the ball."*	◆ Selects and looks at picture books, names pictured objects within one picture.	◆ Intentionally stacks blocks or rings in order of size.	◆ Points to and names four to six colors.	◆ Names some letters and numerals.
◆ Responds to and imitates facial expression.	◆ Recognizes familiar objects; *Ex. "Show me the baby".*	◆ Matches and uses associated objects meaningfully; *Ex. Given cup, saucer, and bead, puts cup and saucer together.*	◆ Draws somewhat recognizable picture that is meaningful to child if not to adult.	◆ Matches picture of familiar objects; *Ex. shoe, sock, foot; apple, orange, banana.*	◆ Rote counts to 10.
◆ Responds to very simple directions; *Ex. raises arms when someone says "Come" and turns head when asked "Where is Daddy?"*	◆ Recognizes self as cause of events; *Ex. turning on a light.*	◆ Stacks rings on peg in order of size.	◆ Names and briefly explains picture.	◆ Draws a person with two to six recognizable parts, such as head, arms, legs.	◆ Sorts objects by single characteristics; *Ex. by color, shape, or size if the difference is obvious.*
◆ Imitates gestures and actions; *Ex. shakes head "no," waves bye-bye.*	◆ Demonstrates active learning; *Ex. explores environment.*	◆ Recognizes self in mirror, saying "baby" or own name.	◆ Asks questions for information; *why* and *how* questions requiring simple answers.	◆ Can name or match drawn parts to own body.	◆ Is beginning to use accurately time concept of *tomorrow* and *yesterday.*
◆ Puts small objects in and out of container with intention.	◆ Is able to match two similar objects.	◆ Can talk briefly about what he or she is doing.	◆ Knows own age.	◆ Draws, names, and describes recognizable picture.	◆ Begins to relate clock time to daily schedule.
	◆ Is able to match two similar objects; *Ex. "Find one like this one."*		◆ Knows own last name.	◆ Rote counts to 5, imitating adults.	◆ Attends to task without distraction.
			◆ Has short attention span.		◆ Begins to sequence events in logical order; i.e., temporal ordering.

(continued)

Cognitive Skills *(continued)*

0 to 12 Months	13 to 24 Months	25 to 36 Months	37 to 48 Months	49 to 60 Months	61 to 72 Months
		◆ Imitates adult actions; *Ex. housekeeping play.* ◆ Understands functional concepts; *Ex. a spoon is used for eating.* ◆ Understands part/whole concepts; *Ex. parts of the body.* ◆ Understands some parts of the body; *Ex. arms, legs.*	◆ Learns through observing and imitating adults, and by adult instruction and explanation. Is very easily distracted. ◆ Has increased understanding of concepts of the functions and groupings of objects; *Ex. can put dollhouse furniture in correct rooms.* ◆ Has increased understanding of part/whole concepts; *Ex. can identify pictures of hand and foot as parts of body.* ◆ Begins to be aware of past and present *Ex. "Yesterday we went to the park. Today we go to the library."*	◆ Knows own street and town. ◆ Observes and listens to adults. ◆ Describes function or use of objects in addition to names of objects. ◆ The child can talk about yesterday or last week. ◆ Understands the concepts of function, time as part/whole relationships.	

Self-help Skills

0 to 12 Months	13 to 24 Months	25 to 36 Months	37 to 48 Months	49 to 60 Months	61 to 72 Months
◆ Child anticipates feeding. ◆ Takes strained food and swallows. ◆ Drinks from cup with assistance. ◆ Feeds self cracker. ◆ Feeds self with fingers.	◆ Uses spoon, spilling little. ◆ Drinks from cup, one hand, unassisted. ◆ Cooperates with dressing; *Ex. holds out arm.* ◆ Removes simple articles; *Ex. mittens.* ◆ Distinguishes between food and nonfood substances.	◆ Uses spoon, with little spilling. ◆ Pours own drink from pitcher. ◆ Opens door by turning handle. ◆ Takes off coat. ◆ Puts on coat with assistance. ◆ Washes and dries hands.	◆ Pours well from small pitcher. ◆ Spreads soft butter with knife. ◆ Buttons and unbuttons large buttons. ◆ Takes care of own toilet needs. ◆ Washes hands unassisted. ◆ Blows nose when reminded.	◆ Cuts soft foods with a knife. ◆ Dresses and undresses without supervision. ◆ Laces shoes.	◆ Dresses self completely. ◆ Ties bow. ◆ Brushes teeth unassisted. ◆ Crosses street safely. ◆ Answers "What to do if" questions involving personal responsibility; *Ex. "What do you do if the fire alarm sounds?"*

Source: BRIGANCE® Diagnostic Inventory of Early Development. Copyright © 1991 Curriculum Associates®, Inc. Reprinted/Adapted by permission.

Social Skills

0 to 12 Months	13 to 24 Months	25 to 36 Months	37 to 48 Months	49 to 60 Months	61 to 72 Months
◆ Looks attentively at a human face. ◆ Smiles spontaneously. ◆ Responds differently to strangers than to familiar people. ◆ Pays attention to own name. ◆ Responds to "No." ◆ Plays simple games; *Ex. Peek-a-boo.*	◆ Recognizes self in mirror or picture. ◆ Responds to adult praise. ◆ Plays by self, initiates own play. ◆ Helps put things away. ◆ Defends own possessions.	◆ Plays near other children. ◆ Watches other children, joins in briefly in their play. ◆ Engages in adult role playing; *Ex. dramatizing mother/father role.* ◆ Symbolically uses objects, self in play; *Ex. acts out simple stories.* ◆ Participates in simple group activity; *Ex. sings, claps, dances.* ◆ Knows gender identity.	◆ Joins in play with other children. ◆ Begins to interact. ◆ Shares toys. ◆ Takes turns with assistance. ◆ Begins dramatic play, acting out whole scenes; *Ex. traveling, playing hours, pretending to be animals.*	◆ Plays and interacts with other children. ◆ Dramatic play is closer to reality, with attention paid to detail, time, and space. ◆ Plays dress-up. ◆ Shows interest in exploring sex differences.	◆ Initiates social contacts and interpretations with peers. ◆ Plays simple table games. ◆ Plays competitive games. ◆ Engages with other children in cooperative play involving group decisions, role assignments—fair play. ◆ Recognizes the feelings of others.

Source: *BRIGANCE® Diagnostic Inventory of Early Development.* Copyright © 1991 Curriculum Associates®, Inc. Reprinted/Adapted by permission.

CHILD DEVELOPMENT CHECKLIST

This checklist is intended as a guide to effective, responsive planning. This is not an assessment tool.

Gross Motor Skills   0 to 12 Months

Name of Child:		D.O.B.:
TASK	**DATE OBSERVED**	**COMMENTS**
1. Lifts head and holds for 5 seconds while lying on stomach.		
2. Holds head steady when held upright for at least 15 seconds while adult walks around.		
3. Rolls from back to side.		
4. Sits without support, without prompting.		
5. Crawls at least 2 feet alternating hands and feet while stomach is up off floor.		
6. Pulls self to standing and stands unaided.		
7. Walks with aid.		
8. Squats to pick up object and returns to standing without falling.		

Gross Motor Skills   **13 to 24 Months**

Name of Child:		D.O.B.:

TASK	DATE OBSERVED	COMMENTS
1. Walks alone; at least 3 steps.		
2. Pulls toy, pushes toy.		
3. Walks without support for 10 feet without falling.		
4. Moves from sitting to standing without support from object or person.		
5. Walks up and down stairs not alternating feet (hand held).		
6. Kicks ball forward without falling.		
7. Moves to music.		
8. Runs forward well.		

Gross Motor Skills   25 to 36 Months

Name of Child:		D.O.B.:

TASK	DATE OBSERVED	COMMENTS
1. Jumps in place, two feet together and remains standing.		
2. Stands on one foot, with aid.		
3. Walks on tiptoe 3 steps.		

Gross Motor Skills   **37 to 48 Months**

Name of Child:		D.O.B.:	
TASK	**DATE OBSERVED**		**COMMENTS**
1. Runs, changing directions.			
2. Walks in a straight line.			
3. Balances on one foot for 5 to 10 seconds.			
4. Hops on one foot.			
5. Pushes, pulls, and steers wheeled toys.			
6. Rides (steers and pedals) tricycle.			
7. Uses slide without assistance.			
8. Jumps over 6-inch- (15 cm.) high object landing on both feet together.			
9. Throws ball overhand.			
10. Catches ball bounced to him or her.			
11. Walks up and down stairs alone alternating feet.			

Gross Motor Skills   49 to 60 Months

Name of Child:		D.O.B.:	
TASK	**DATE OBSERVED**	**COMMENTS**	
1. Walks backward toe-heel.			
2. Jumps forward 10 times without falling.			
3. Jumps over rope positioned at child's midcalf.			
4. Turns somersault.			

Gross Motor Skills   **61 to 72 Months**

Name of Child:		D.O.B.:
TASK	**DATE OBSERVED**	**COMMENTS**
1. Catches ball at distance of 5 feet.		
2. Walks on balance beam.		
3. Can cover 6½ feet (2 meters) hopping on one foot.		
4. Skips on alternate feet.		
5. Jumps rope.		
6. Skates.		

Fine Motor Skills   0 to 12 Months

Name of Child:		D.O.B.:	
TASK	**DATE OBSERVED**	**COMMENTS**	
1. Reaches, grasps, objects in mouth.			
2. Picks things up with fingers against heel of palm (Palmer grasp).			
3. Transfers object from one hand to other hand.			
4. Drops and picks up toy.			

Fine Motor Skills   **13 to 24 Months**

Name of Child:		D.O.B.:
TASK	**DATE OBSERVED**	**COMMENTS**
1. Picks up things with thumb and index finger.		
2. Builds tower of three small blocks.		
3. Puts four rings on stick.		
4. Places five pegs in pegboard.		
5. Turns pages two or three pages at a time.		
6. Random scribbles without direction.		
7. Throws small ball at least 3 feet.		
8. Paints with whole arm movement, shifts hands, makes strokes.		

Fine Motor Skills   25 to 36 Months

Name of Child:		D.O.B.:
TASK	**DATE OBSERVED**	**COMMENTS**
1. Turns knobs.		
2. Strings large beads.		
3. Turns pages singly of a primary book.		
4. Holds crayon with thumb and fingers, not fist.		
5. Uses one hand consistently in most activities.		
6. Paints with some wrist actions, makes dots, lines, circular strokes.		
7. Rolls, pounds, squeezes, and pulls clay.		
8. Cuts paper in two with scissors.		

Fine Motor Skills   37 to 48 Months

Name of Child: D.O.B.:

TASK	DATE OBSERVED	COMMENTS
1. Uses one hand consistently.		
2. Builds tower of nine small blocks.		
3. Drives nails and pegs.		
4. Copies circle.		
5. Manipulates clay materials (for example: rolls balls, snakes, cookies).		

Fine Motor Skills   49 to 60 Months

Name of Child:		D.O.B.:	
TASK	**DATE OBSERVED**	**COMMENTS**	
1. Cuts on line continuously.			
2. Copies cross.			
3. Copies square.			
4. Prints a few capital letters.			

Fine Motor Skills   **61 to 72 Months**

Name of Child:		D.O.B.:
TASK	**DATE OBSERVED**	**COMMENTS**
1. Cuts out simple shapes: triangle, circle, square.		
2. Copies first name.		
3. Prints numerals 1–5.		
4. Colors within lines.		
5. Has handedness well established (that is, child is left- or right-handed).		
6. Pastes and glues appropriately.		

Literacy/Expressive Language   0 to 12 Months

Name of Child:		D.O.B.:
TASK	**DATE OBSERVED**	**COMMENTS**
1. Makes crying and non-crying sounds.		
2. Repeats some vowel and consonant sounds (babbles) when alone or when spoken to.		
3. Interacts with others by vocalizing after adult.		
4. Communicates meaning through intonation; *Ex. Sound is more distinct.*		
5. Attempts to imitate speech sounds; *Ex. "Bye-bye."*		

Literacy/Expressive Language   **13 to 24 Months**

Name of Child:		D.O.B.:
TASK	**DATE OBSERVED**	**COMMENTS**
1. Says first meaningful word.		
2. Uses single words plus a gesture to indicate wants or needs.		
3. Refers to self by name.		
4. Uses *my* and *mine* to indicate possession.		
5. Says successive words to describe an event.		
6. Has vocabulary of about 20 words for people and common objects.		

Literacy/Expressive Language 25 to 36 Months

Name of Child:		D.O.B.:	
TASK	**DATE OBSERVED**	**COMMENTS**	
1. Joins vocabulary words together in two-word phrases.			
2. Gives first and last name.			
3. Asks *what* and *where* questions.			
4. Makes negative statements; *Ex. Can't open it.*			
5. Shows frustration at not being understood.			

Literacy/Expressive Language   37 to 48 Months

Name of Child:	D.O.B.:	
TASK	**DATE OBSERVED**	**COMMENTS**
1. Talks in sentences of three or more words, which take the form agent-action-location. *Ex. "Daddy, sit on chair."*		
2. Tells about past experiences.		
3. Uses *s* on nouns to indicate plurals.		
4. Uses *ed* on verbs to indicate past tense.		
5. Repeats at least one nursery rhyme and can sing a song.		
6. Speech is understandable to strangers, but there is still some sound error.		

Literacy/Expressive Language   49 to 60 Months

Name of Child:		D.O.B.:	
TASK	**DATE OBSERVED**	**COMMENTS**	
1. Asks *when, how,* and *why* questions.			
2. Talks about causality by using *because* and *so*.			
3. Tells the content of a story but may confuse facts.			

Literacy/Expressive Language   **61 to 72 Months**

Name of Child:		D.O.B.:
TASK	**DATE OBSERVED**	**COMMENTS**
1. Child engages in meaningful dialogue; *Ex. Gives and receives information.*		
2. Uses irregular past tense verbs; *Ex. I spoke; I drank.*		
3. Communicates his/her feelings.		

Literacy/Receptive Language   0 to 12 Months

Name of Child:		D.O.B.:
TASK	**DATE OBSERVED**	**COMMENTS**
1. Responds to speech by looking at speaker.		
2. Responds differently to aspects of speaker's voice; *Ex. Friendly or unfriendly, male or female.*		
3. Turns to source of sound.		
4. Responds with gesture to *hi, bye-bye,* and *up* when these words are accompanied by appropriate gesture and tone.		

Literacy/Receptive Language   **13 to 24 Months**

Name of Child:		D.O.B.:
TASK	**DATE OBSERVED**	**COMMENTS**
1. Understands simple phrases; *Ex. "Open the door," "Get the ball."*		
2. Responds verbally or non-verbally when asked *where* when question is accompanied by gesture. *Ex. "Where is the dog?"*		
3. Understands prepositions *on, in, under.*		
4. Follows request to bring familiar object from another room.		
5. Follows a series of two simple, but related directions.		

Literacy/Receptive Language   **25 to 36 Months**

Name of Child:		D.O.B.:	
TASK	**DATE OBSERVED**	**COMMENTS**	
1. Can identify objects when told their use; *Ex. "Show me the one you brush your teeth with."*			
2. Understands question forms *what* and *where*.			
3. Understands negatives— *no, not, can't, don't.*			
4. Enjoys listening to simple storybooks and requests them again.			

Literacy/Receptive Language   37 to 48 Months

Name of Child:		D.O.B.:
TASK	**DATE OBSERVED**	**COMMENTS**
1. Understands size comparisons such as *big* and *bigger*.		
2. Understands relationships expressed by *if ..., then* or *because* sentences.		
3. Carries out a series of two to four related directions.		
4. Understands when told "Let's pretend."		

Literacy/Receptive Language   49 to 60 Months

Name of Child:		D.O.B.:	
TASK	**DATE OBSERVED**	**COMMENTS**	
1. Understands comparatives like *big, bigger, biggest.*			
2. Understands the use of plurals; *Ex. "Bring me the books."*			
3. Understands sequencing of events when told them; *Ex. "First we have to go to the store, then we can make the cake, and tomorrow we will eat it."*			

Literacy/Receptive Language   **61 to 72 Months**

Name of Child:		D.O.B.:
TASK	**DATE OBSERVED**	**COMMENTS**
1. Recalls events from story presented orally without pictures.		
2. Follows three unrelated directions; *Ex. Put the cup in the sink; Pick up the ball; Sit on the couch.*		

Cognitive Skills   0 to 12 Months

Name of Child:		D.O.B.:
TASK	**DATE OBSERVED**	**COMMENTS**
1. Child shows awareness of new situations; *Ex. Showing surprise.*		
2. Responds to strangers by crying or staring.		
3. Responds to and imitates facial expression.		
4. Responds to very simple directions; *Ex. Raises arms when someone says "Come" and turns head when asked "Where is Daddy?"*		
5. Imitates gestures and actions; *Ex. Shakes head "no," waves "bye-bye."*		
6. Puts small objects in and out of container with intention.		

Cognitive Skills   **13 to 24 Months**

Name of Child:		D.O.B.:

TASK	DATE OBSERVED	COMMENTS
1. Imitates actions and words of adults.		
2. Responds to words or commands with appropriate actions; *Ex. "Give me the ball."*		
3. Recognizes familiar objects; *Ex. "Show me the baby."*		
4. Recognizes self as cause of events; *Ex. Turning on a light.*		
5. Demonstrates active learning; *Ex. Explores environment.*		
6. Is able to match two similar objects.		
7. Is able to match two similar objects; *Ex. "Find one like this one."*		

Cognitive Skills   25 to 36 Months

Name of Child:		D.O.B.:

TASK	DATE OBSERVED	COMMENTS
1. Responds to simple directions; *Ex.* *"Give me the ball and block." "Get your shoes and socks."*		
2. Selects and looks at picture books, names pictured objects within one picture.		
3. Matches and uses associated objects meaningfully; *Ex. Given cup, saucer, and bead, puts cup and saucer together.*		
4. Stacks rings on peg in order of size.		
5. Recognizes self in mirror, saying "baby" or own name.		
6. Can talk briefly about what he or she is doing.		
7. Imitates adult actions; *Ex. Housekeeping play.*		
8. Understands functional concepts; *Ex. A spoon is used for eating.*		
9. Understands part/whole concepts; *Ex. Parts of the body.*		
10. Understands some parts of the body; *Ex. Arms, legs.*		

Cognitive Skills   ## 37 to 48 Months

Name of Child:	D.O.B.:	
TASK	**DATE OBSERVED**	**COMMENTS**
1. Recognizes and matches six colors.		
2. Intentionally stacks blocks or rings in order of size.		
3. Draws somewhat recognizable picture that is meaningful to child if not to adult.		
4. Names and briefly explains picture.		
5. Asks questions for information; *why* and *how* questions requiring simple answers.		
6. Knows own age.		
7. Knows own last name.		
8. Has short attention span.		
9. Learns through observing and imitating adults, and by adult instruction and explanation. Is very easily distracted.		
10. Has increased understanding of concepts of the functions and groupings of objects; *Ex. Can put doll house furniture in correct rooms.*		
11. Has increased understanding of part/whole concepts; *Ex. Can identify pictures of hand and foot as parts of body.*		
12. Begins to be aware of past and present *Ex. "Yesterday we went to the park. Today we go to the library."*		

Cognitive Skills   49 to 60 Months

Name of Child:		D.O.B.:

TASK	DATE OBSERVED	COMMENTS
1. Plays with words; creates own rhyming words; says or makes words having similar sounds.		
2. Points to and names four to six colors.		
3. Matches picture of familiar objects; *Ex. Shoe, sock, foot; apple, orange, banana.*		
4. Draws a person with two to six recognizable parts, such as head, arms, legs.		
5. Can name or match drawn parts to own body.		
6. Draws, names, and describes recognizable picture.		
7. Rote counts to 5, imitating adults.		
8. Knows own street and town.		
9. Observes and listens to adults.		
10. Describes function or use of objects in addition to names of objects.		
11. The child can talk about yesterday or last week.		
12. Understands the concepts of function, time as part/ whole relationships.		

Cognitive Skills   **61 to 72 Months**

Name of Child:		D.O.B.:	
TASK	**DATE OBSERVED**	**COMMENTS**	
1. Selects single word from visual presentation.			
2. Names some letters and numerals.			
3. Rote counts to 10.			
4. Sorts objects by single characteristics; *Ex. By color, shape, or size if the difference is obvious.*			
5. Is beginning to use accurately time concept of *tomorrow* and *yesterday.*			
6. Begins to relate clock time to daily schedule.			
7. Attends to task without distraction.			
8. Begins to sequence events in logical order; i.e., temporal ordering.			

Self-help Skills   0 to 12 Months

Name of Child:		D.O.B.:
TASK	**DATE OBSERVED**	**COMMENTS**
1. Child anticipates feeding.		
2. Takes strained food and swallows.		
3. Drinks from cup with assistance.		
4. Feeds self cracker.		
5. Feeds self with fingers.		

Self-help Skills   13 to 24 Months

Name of Child:		D.O.B.:
TASK	**DATE OBSERVED**	**COMMENTS**
1. Uses spoon, spilling little.		
2. Drinks from cup, one hand, unassisted.		
3. Cooperates with dressing; *Ex. Holds out arm.*		
4. Removes simple articles; *Ex. Mittens.*		
5. Distinguishes between food and nonfood substances.		

Self-help Skills   25 to 36 Months

Name of Child:		D.O.B.:
TASK	**DATE OBSERVED**	**COMMENTS**
1. Uses spoon, with little spilling.		
2. Pours own drink from pitcher.		
3. Opens door by turning handle.		
4. Takes off coat.		
5. Puts on coat with assistance.		
6. Washes and dries hands.		

Self-help Skills   **37 to 48 Months**

Name of Child:		D.O.B.:
TASK	**DATE OBSERVED**	**COMMENTS**
1. Pours well from small pitcher.		
2. Spreads soft butter with knife.		
3. Buttons and unbuttons large buttons.		
4. Takes care of own toilet needs.		
5. Washes hands unassisted.		
6. Blows nose when reminded.		

Self-help Skills   49 to 60 Months

Name of Child:		D.O.B.:
TASK	**DATE OBSERVED**	**COMMENTS**
1. Cuts soft foods with a knife.		
2. Dresses and undresses without supervision.		
3. Laces shoes.		

Self-help Skills   61 to 72 Months

Name of Child:		D.O.B.:
TASK	**DATE OBSERVED**	**COMMENTS**
1. Dresses self completely.		
2. Ties bow.		
3. Brushes teeth unassisted.		
4. Crosses street safely.		
5. Answers "What to do if" questions involving personal responsibility; *Ex.* *"What do you do if the fire alarm sounds?"*		

Self-help Skills

Social Skills   0 to 12 Months

Name of Child:		D.O.B.:
TASK	**DATE OBSERVED**	**COMMENTS**
1. Looks attentively at a human face.		
2. Smiles spontaneously.		
3. Responds differently to strangers than to familiar people.		
4. Pays attention to own name.		
5. Responds to "No."		
6. Plays simple games; *Ex. Peek-a-boo.*		

Social Skills   **13 to 24 Months**

Name of Child:		D.O.B.:
TASK	**DATE OBSERVED**	**COMMENTS**
1. Recognizes self in mirror or picture.		
2. Responds to adult praise.		
3. Plays by self, initiates own play.		
4. Helps put things away.		
5. Defends own possessions.		

Social Skills   **25 to 36 Months**

Name of Child:		D.O.B.:
TASK	**DATE OBSERVED**	**COMMENTS**
1. Plays near other children.		
2. Watches other children, joins in briefly in their play.		
3. Engages in adult role playing; *Ex. Dramatizing mother/father role.*		
4. Symbolically uses objects, self in play; *Ex. Acts out simple stories.*		
5. Participates in simple group activity; *Ex. Sings, claps, dances.*		
6. Knows gender identity.		

Social Skills   **37 to 48 Months**

Name of Child:		D.O.B.:
TASK	**DATE OBSERVED**	**COMMENTS**
1. Joins in play with other children.		
2. Begins to interact.		
3. Shares toys.		
4. Takes turns with assistance.		
5. Begins dramatic play, acting out whole scenes; *Ex. Traveling, playing hours, pretending to be animals.*		

Social Skills   49 to 60 Months

Name of Child:		D.O.B.:
TASK	**DATE OBSERVED**	**COMMENTS**
1. Plays and interacts with other children.		
2. Dramatic play is closer to reality, with attention paid to detail, time, and space.		
3. Plays dress-up.		
4. Shows interest in exploring sex differences.		

Social Skills   61 to 72 Months

Name of Child:		D.O.B.:
TASK	**DATE OBSERVED**	**COMMENTS**
1. Initiates social contacts and interpretations with peers.		
2. Plays simple table games.		
3. Plays competitive games.		
4. Engages with other children in cooperative play involving group decisions, role assignments—fair play.		
5. Recognizes the feelings of others.		

APPENDIX C:
Guidance Checklist

Building relationships with children requires the adult to consider important aspects of guiding behavior.

A Guidance Checklist is a useful tool that can become a mental checklist for quick reference.

Before I intervene:

1. What is the worst thing that can happen?

2. Who has the problem?

3. Am I in control and aware of myself? (facial expression, body language, tone of voice)

4. Have I considered the child's individuality and specific needs?

5. Will the strategy that I have chosen preserve the child's self-respect?

6. Does the child understand my expectations? (or limits?)

7. Is the child developmentally able to understand the consequences?

8. Is the technique chosen developmentally appropriate for this child?

9. Am I being fair?

10. Do I have the language tools?

11. Am I offering meaningful choices?

12. Is this strategy promoting my goal of self-discipline?

APPENDIX D:
Infant/Toddler
Information Record

Child's Name:			
What did your child have for breakfast?			
How did your child sleep?			
Preschooler's health:			
Parent's special instructions for the day:			
Caregiver's Name:			

FOOD INTAKE

A.M. snacks:

Lunch:

P.M. Snacks:

DIAPER CHANGES

URINATIONS	STOOLS	COMMENTS

Sleep or Rest Time Comments:

CHILD'S DAY—Areas of interest, social experiences, etc.

NEEDS:	Diapers:	Wipes:
	Diaper Cream:	Other:

APPENDIX E:
Curriculum Planning Sheets

CURRICULUM WEBBING

One of the popular methods of curriculum planning is curriculum webbing. This concept allows the Educator to brainstorm ideas, which include the interests expressed by the child, and then build connections from the ideas with learning outcomes and a learning focus or theme.

Observing the children and analyzing their developmental needs are essential to determine the direction of programming in creating a web.

Creating a Curriculum Web

Step 1

Identify concepts from children's interests that are:
- drawn from real life.
- related to child's prior experience.
- drawn from the here and now.

Step 2

Teachers brainstorm each topic (concept), listing as many heading and subheadings as possible.

Step 3

Integrate concepts with the goals and learner outcomes in a flowchart formation.

Step 4

Decide where to start, the materials required, and the experiences to invite the child to take part. Interface concepts and learner outcomes with all the established domains.

Objectives will reflect developmentally appropriate practices regarding **physical**, **cognitive**, **social**, and **emotional** needs of the child.

PLANNING SHEETS

Concept Focus: _____ Week of: _____

AREA	MONDAY	TUESDAY	WEDNESDAY	THURSDAY	FRIDAY
Language					
Cognitive					
Music					
Sensory					
Art					
Construction					

PLANNING SHEETS

Concept Focus: _____ Week of: _____

AREA	MONDAY	TUESDAY	WEDNESDAY	THURSDAY	FRIDAY
Gross Motor / Fine Motor					
Outdoor					
Science/Discovery					
Dramatic Play					
Field Trip/Outings					

PLANNING SHEETS

Concept Focus: _____ Week of: _____

AREA	MONDAY	TUESDAY	WEDNESDAY	THURSDAY	FRIDAY
Investigations, Projects					
Materials to Add/ Delete/Change					
Goals					

APPENDIX F:
Diversity, Anti-Bias[1] Checklists

GOALS: PROGRAM AND TEACHER

Does the Program and Teacher —	Yes	No
1. Foster multiculturalism, self-worth, a sense of dignity and unity, and understand that to be different is not to be inferior?		
2. Accept the uniqueness of each child, his/her cultural background and recognize that each has something valuable to contribute?		
3. Use the child's experiences to teach the other children?		
4. Develop and encourage the teacher-learner model, where the teacher and the child learn from each other?		
5. Combine the teaching of skills with the teaching of multiculturalism, and recognize that these do not need to be taught separately?		
6. Understand that all children bring with them valuable bases from which learning can occur, and understand the children's backgrounds to enhance the teacher-learner model?		
7. Develop an atmosphere in the classroom that encourages cooperation and unity and the sharing of individual experiences?		
8. Present the children with objective materials about different cultures, instead of only those materials that have been prepared through the viewpoint of the dominant group? (They should include books, posters, and similar elements.)		
9. Help the teacher become aware of his or her own prejudices and biases?		
10. Understand that learning abilities, cognitive styles, and expectations vary among cultures and that these may have a significant impact on the teaching methods and curriculum plan?		

(continued)

---

[1] *Source:* Compiled by Valerie Rhomberg.

GOALS: CHILDREN

Are Children Encouraged to —	Yes	No
1. Become aware of one's own uniqueness? (This may include body features, language, culture, and background.)		
2. Become familiar with one's own historical roots as well as those of the group and the community?		
3. Accept the differences of others and realize that being different does not mean that one is inferior?		
4. Promote equality between and respect for other cultures, and arrest prejudices that breed ignorance?		
5. Encourage freedom of speech and a willingness to share without intimidation, both in one's own and other cultural groups?		
6. Develop a sense of responsibility and belonging to the group, and understand that unity is possible within a diverse group?		

Appendix G:
Safety Checklist

INDOORS	Yes	No	N/A
1. Locks on doors can be opened by an adult or older children without difficulty.			
2. Soiled diapers are disposed of in securely tied plastic bag(s). Soiled diapers and diaper pails must be stored away from children.			
3. There are no precariously placed small, sharp, or otherwise hazardous objects.			
4. Furnishings are in good repair and free of sharp edges, splinters, pinch points, or crush points.			
5. Drapery and blind cords are tied up and secured with safety hooks.			
6. All storage units are well constructed and stable. Units are anchored to the wall or flooring to prevent sliding, collapsing, or tipping over.			
7. All TVs, VCRs, computers, projectors, and the like, are secured on stands that ensure no tipping or collapse.			
8. Dishes are in good condition and not cracked, chipped, or crazed.			
9. Sharp, pointed, or otherwise dangerous cooking utensils such as knives or glass are not within the children's grasp.			
10. Garbage containers have tightly fitted lids; preferably operated by foot pedals. (Lids should not be left up after use.) Do not store containers near a furnace or water heaters (fire hazard).			
11. Cleaning agents are stored in original containers that are properly labeled and kept in a locked cupboard (along with any tools, matches or lighters, and plastic bags) away from any food.			
12. All medication is stored out of reach of children (a locked cupboard or container may be required).			

(continued)

SUPERVISION	Yes	No	N/A
1. Children are never left unattended in the kitchen.			
2. Children are supervised by enough well-trained staff who can evacuate children in an emergency.			
3. There is no bottle-propping.			
4. Toddlers sit down with bottles or food.			
5. Running is encouraged outdoors only unless part of an activity.			

EQUIPMENT	Yes	No	N/A
1. Toys are in good repair and free of sharp edges, pinch points, and splinters.			
2. Toys accessible to young children have strings or cords of 6 inches (15 cm.) except toboggans and pull toys.			
3. Toys are stored when not being used. (Open shelving is desirable for easy selection.)			
4. Toys are age-appropriate and suited to the abilities of the children using them.			

PLAY AND SLEEPING AREAS	Yes	No	N/A
1. All exits are clearly marked and free of any obstacles or clutter.			
2. There is easy access to emergency phones.			
3. Electrical cords are not within children's reach. Cords are not run under carpeting nor are they in traffic paths or doorways.			
4. Unused extension cords are unplugged and out of reach.			
5. Unused electrical outlets have plastic outlet covers.			
6. Drawers are kept closed.			
7. Matches, lighters, medicines, cleaning agents, and tools are inaccessible to children.			
8. Staff and visitors' belongings, purses, and medications are inaccessible to children.			
9. Art materials are properly stored in labeled containers.			

HALLWAYS AND STAIRS	Yes	No	N/A
1. Exits are clearly marked.			
2. Electrical cords are out of children's reach and kept out of doorways and from under carpets. Unused extension cords are unplugged.			
3. Unused electrical outlets at child's level have plastic outlet covers.			

KITCHEN	Yes	No	N/A
1. Pot handles are always turned towards the back of the stove.			
2. Appliance cords are rolled up when not in use. No cords hang over the counter where they could be caught in a cupboard or drawer or be within children's reach. Knives and other sharp utensils are stored safely.			

WASHROOMS	Yes	No	N/A
1. Step stools are provided, where appropriate, for sink and toilet.			
2. Cleaning agents are stored in original containers and kept in a locked cupboard out of children's reach.			
3. Garbage containers have tightly fitting lids, preferably operated by foot pedals. (Lids should not be left up after use.) Garbage containers are emptied daily.			
4. Plastic bags are stored out of children's reach.			
5. Any locked door can easily be opened by an adult.			

OUTDOORS: TRAFFIC/FIELD TRIPS/VEHICLES	Yes	No	N/A
1. Staff are aware of who can take a child out of the child care facility.			
2. Staff are trained in what to do in an emergency; a written plan or procedure is available.			

PLAYGROUND: SUPERVISION	Yes	No	N/A
1. Check with licencing source to ensure that regulations regarding playground maintenance are current.			
2. Full staff-child ratios are to be maintained.			
3. There are a minimum of two adults on the playground (one to deal with emergencies and one to supervise) at all times.			
4. Staff are strategically stationed around the playground and away from each other to effectively monitor children's activity.			
5. Attendance records and a head count of children are accurate at all times.			
6. Staff interact with the children both to enhance play and to keep abreast of potential problems/dangers.			
7. Staff provide supervision to each large play structure.			
8. Programs with odd-shaped playgrounds ensure that effective supervision is in place at all times. Design changes are a primary consideration.			

PLAYGROUND: CLOTHING	Yes	No	N/A
1. Staff require warm, comfortable clothing and foot gear in winter months so that they can participate in children's activities and access children who require assistance.			
2. Children's winter boots often slip on metal and plastic surfaces. Structures that have the potential to be dangerous are made off limits for the children.			
3. In the summer months, running shoes have more flex and grip on structures than vinyl dress shoes or sandals.			
4. Always take off, tie up, or tuck in drawstrings or cords on hoods, hats, jackets, or mittens. Zip up jackets, tuck in scarves, and take precaution with loose clothing, hoods, and toggles that have the potential to get caught on playground equipment.			
5. Children are aware of the need to zip up jackets, tie up strings on hoods, hats, and jackets, and tuck in scarves.			
6. Children are protected from the sun with hats, sun screen, and cool cotton clothing in summer months.			

PLAYGROUND: SPECIAL ACTIVITIES	Yes	No	N/A
1. Winter sliding requires special supervision. The rules should be developed to include: ♦ where the children can slide. ♦ what they can use for sliding. ♦ where and how the children climb the hill. ♦ who controls when the child can start to slide.			
2. For ice skating, parents should be required to provide helmets. Children's broom ball helmets are light-weight and cost less than hockey helmets.			
3. For all excursions and field trips, children's medical information (i.e., for severe allergies) and a first aid kit should be taken along. It is useful to have a backpack designated for this purpose.			

PLAYGROUND: EMERGENCIES	Yes	No	N/A
1. A common occurrence in the winter is for children to stick their tongues on metal. A plastic squirt bottle filled with room temperature water (in the staff member's pocket) can greatly assist in loosening the tongue.			
2. All staff are encouraged to take CPR and First Aid Training.			
3. Ensure that a first aid kit is readily available for the playground.			
4. Ensure that staff are briefed on medical emergencies and the completion of accident reports and serious occurrence reports.			
5. Document and review all accidents that occur. Advise parents of each one, regardless of how insignificant it is.			
6. All accidents or injuries that require medical attention are to be reported to the Program Advisor within 24 hours.			

PLAYGROUND: CHOOSING APPARATUS	Yes	No	N/A
1. Consider equipment that will allow staff to easily reach and assist children in trouble.			
2. Choose climbing apparatus that allows children's feet to touch the ground at the tallest point (or about 4 feet in height).			
3. Utilize lightweight shock-absorbent swing seats.			
4. Avoid equipment with protruding bars inside that could catch children's limbs should they fall.			
5. Rungs on climbers should be placed approximately 1 foot apart rather than 6 inches to 6½ inches.			

PLAYGROUND: EQUIPMENT MAINTENANCE	Yes	No	N/A
1. Check the playground daily for broken glass, animal droppings, snow build-up around fences and structures, and broken equipment.			
2. Remove unsafe or disassembled equipment from the playground.			
3. Conduct constant checks on equipment/apparatus and watch for signs of decay, rust, splinters, sharp protrusions, protruding nuts, bolts, rivets, or nails. Ensure that repairs or adjustments are conducted immediately.			
4. Hard play surfaces should be kept clean of stones, sand, and gravel.			
5. In cold weather, climbing structures need to be checked for frost and ice.			
6. The grass should be kept well groomed.			
7. Sand in the sandbox is to be replaced when it is dirty or contaminated.			
8. All climbing structures require an absorbent material under and around them.			
9. Ensure that snow is shoveled away from the base of climbing equipment and fencing so that it does not build up to allow children to reach dangerous heights and positions that they normally could not get into. Gates should easily open.			
10. Remove cords, string, or skipping ropes tied to slides, swings, or other playground equipment. Make children aware of the dangers these items pose.			

KEEP PARENTS INFORMED	Yes	No	N/A
1. Talk to parents about children's clothing and discuss the possible dangers of drawstrings, toggles, scarves, mitten cords, and other items placed around the neck on a string catching on equipment and preventing a quick and safe escape.			
2. Share product-safety information such as the enclosed information/fact sheets and other topics of relevance with parents.			
3. Provide parents with safety related information through handouts, newsletters, and in "Parents Handbooks." Information may be obtained by contacting: Canadian Standards Association 178 Rexdale Blvd. Etobicoke, ON M9R 1R3 Canada			

UNIVERSAL PRECAUTIONS	Yes	No	N/A
1. Wash hands immediately after exposure to blood.			
2. Cover cuts.			
3. Use absorbent materials to stop bleeding.			
4. Wear disposable gloves when there is a lot of blood or if you have open cuts. Wash hands immediately after removing gloves.			
5. Immediately clean blood-soiled surfaces and disinfect with bleach solution. (Household bleach kills HIV.)			
6. Machine wash blood-stained laundry separately in hot soapy water.			
7. Place blood-stained materials in sealed plastic bags and discard in lined, covered garbage containers.			

With the permission of Canadian Standards Association, material is reproduced from CSA Standard CAN/CSA-Z614-98, Children's Playspaces and Equipment, which is copyrighted by Canadian Standards Association, 178 Rexdale Blvd., Toronto, Ontario, M9W 1R3. While use of this material has been authorized, CSA shall not be responsible for the manner in which the information is presented, nor for any interpretations thereof.

APPENDIX H:
Weekly Checklist Evaluation

WEEKLY CHECKLIST EVALUATION			
Week Ending:	**Satisfactory**	**Needs Improvement**	**Comments**
COGNITIVE DOMAIN			
Science Display:			
Sand/Water:			
Block Play:			
Activities:			
AESTHETIC DOMAIN			
Dramatic Area:			
Arts:			
Music:			
LANGUAGE DOMAIN			
Stories:			
Puppets:			
Poetry:			
Word Games:			
PHYSICAL DOMAIN			
Gross Motor:			
Snacks and Lunches:			

(continued)

WEEKLY CHECKLIST EVALUATION		
	Done	**Comments**
OTHER		
Changing Toys/Books:		
Changing Pictures and/or Bulletin Boards:		
Field Trips: Record:		
Visitors to Program: Record:		
Playground Activities: Record:		
Information Boards:		
Newsletters:		

WEEKLY CHECKLIST EVALUATION			
	Satisfactory	Needs Improvement	Comments
PHYSICAL SET-UP			
◆ The space is inviting to children.			
◆ The space is divided into well-defined interest areas to encourage distinctive types of play.			
◆ The space incorporates places for group activities, eating, resting, and storing children's belongings.			
◆ Interest areas are arranged to promote visibility and easy movement between areas.			
◆ Interest areas are flexible to accommodate practical considerations and children's changing interests.			
◆ Materials are plentiful and support a wide range of play experiences.			
◆ Materials reflect children's family lives.			
◆ The storage of material promotes the find-use-return cycle.			

Appendix I:
Action Plan

ACTION PLAN – PERSONAL/PROFESSIONAL GOALS				
Name:			Date:	
Goals	Tasks	Resources Required	Time Line	Comments

ACTION PLAN — PROGRAM GOALS

Name:

Date:

Goals	Tasks	Resources Required	Time Line	Comments

References

Appendix B: Child Development Chart
Brigance, A. H. (1991). *Diagnostic inventory of early development*. North Billerica, MA: Curriculum Associates®, Inc.

Appendix F: Diversity, Anti-Bias Checklist
Hall, N. S., Rhomberg, V. (1995). *Effective curriculum: Teaching the anti-bias approach*. Nelson Canada.

Appendix G: Safety Checklist
Canadian Standards Association. (1999). *Children's playspaces and equipment*. 178 Rexdale Blvd., Etobicoke, ON, M9R 1R3, Canada.

Brain Development: Importance in the Early Years
McCain, Hon. M. N., Mustard, Dr. J. Fraser. (1999). *Early years study: Reversing the real brain drain*. Toronto, ON, Canada: Government of Ontario, Canada.

Guy, K. A. (Ed.) (1997). *Our promise to children*. Ottawa, ON, Canada: Canadian Institute of Child Health.

Cognitive and Language/Literacy Domain
Queen's Printer for Ontario. (1998). *The kindergarten program*. Ministry of Education and Training. Toronto, ON, Canada: Government of Ontario.

Professional Development in the Lives of Early Childhood Educators
Katz, L. G. (1977). *Talks with teachers: Reflections on early childhood education*. Washington, DC: National Association for the Education of Young Children.

Willer, B. (Ed.) (1993). *A conceptual framework for early childhood professional development* (NAEYC position statement). Washington, DC: National Association for the Education of Young Children.

Self Assessment/Reflection and Action Planning
Baptiste, N. (1994). "Always growing and learning." *Daycare and Early Education*, Winter (pp. 26–29).

Duff, R. E., Brown, M. H., Van Scoy, I. J. (1995). "Reflection and self evaluation: Keys to professional development." *Young Children*, May (pp. 81–83).

Teacher-Child Ratios
Bredecamp, S., Copple, C. (Eds.) (1997). *Developmentally appropriate practice in early childhood programs* (pp. 80, 90, 135, 177–8). Washington, DC: National Association for the Education of Young Children.